Eradication

Poet-activist Mayyu Ali has been campaigning for years to denounce the genocide of his community, the Rohingyas. While living in the refugee camps of Bangladesh, he opened several schools for Rohingya youth and children. He has been part of several award-winning documentaries by BBC, and others, and works with multiple NGOs. In 2019, he co-founded The Art Garden Rohingya, a Rohingya art and poetry project. He has also published two books in English, *Exodus* and *The White Elephant*.

In 2024, he graduated with a Master of Arts in Global Governance from the University of Waterloo. Currently, he is serving as a director of the Rohingya Language Preservation Project of Community Rebuilding Centre, seeking to preserve Rohingya language and culture which are at high risk of extinction in the face of genocide in Myanmar and displacement in Bangladesh and other southeast Asian countries.

Emilie Lopes is a French reporter. She has collaborated with numerous newspapers such as *Le Figaro*, *ELLE*, *L'Obs* and so on.

Siba Barkataki is an assistant professor at the English and Foreign Languages University, Hyderabad. Her areas of specialization include Francophone Literature, Indian Indenture Studies and Memory Studies. In 2010, she received the prestigious Swiss Government Excellence Scholarship and in 2015, she was awarded a UGC postdoctoral fellowship for her research in the field of Indian Indenture Studies.

Eradication

A POET AT THE HEART OF THE
ROHINGYA GENOCIDE

MAYYU ALI
with EMILIE LOPES

Translated from the French by SIBA BARKATAKI

PAN

First published in French as *L'Effacement* 2022 by Éditions Grasset & Fasquelle
First published in English 2025 by Pan
an imprint of Pan Macmillan Publishing India Private Limited
707 Kailash Building
26 K. G. Marg, New Delhi 110001
www.panmacmillan.co.in

Pan Macmillan, The Smithson, 6 Briset Street, Farringdon, London EC1M 5NR
Associated companies throughout the world
www.panmacmillan.com

ISBN 978-93-6113-613-9

1 3 5 7 9 8 6 4 2

Typeset in Dante MT Std by R. Ajith Kumar, New Delhi
Printed and bound in India by Replika Press Pvt. Ltd.

FSC www.fsc.org
MIX
Paper | Supporting responsible forestry
FSC™ C016779

To my grandfather, Ali Akbar

To my mentor, Mohib Ullah, assassinated during the writing of this book

To the Rohingyas who had to let go of their lands

To those who were mercilessly massacred

To those who were raped and tortured

To the brave women and men who survived and are now fighting for justice to be served

And to those who are hoping to go back to Myanmar for a better future

'Zoaw haile haiyaw, himmat no haraiyaw.'

'Nourish yourself, with rice gruel if need be, but don't ever lose your courage.'

A Rohingya proverb

This book contains explicit
descriptions of genocide,
sexual violence, and death.
Reader discretion is advised.

Foreword

THIS BOOK NEARLY DIDN'T see the light of day. Two years ago, when we had just finished writing it, we were forced to suspend its publication indefinitely. Mayyu Ali's life was at stake. An armed group had sworn to kill him if he continued to condemn and testify against the crimes committed in the Bangladeshi refugee camps. As an initial warning, his brother was abducted and some of his contacts went missing. Fearing the worst, Mayyu had to resign himself to a clandestine life until August 2021, when he could finally take the path of exile with his wife and daughter, and the publication of this book was once again possible.

All the while – despite the threats and the fear that consumed him – Mayyu refused to give in. The publication of his story was the need of the hour, and coming to France to meet his future readers was a dream that we began trying to turn into reality with the help of Éditions Grasset, several governments, the UN High

Commissioner for Refugees, Amnesty International and Fortify Rights. One had to be a little crazy to believe that this was even possible. Mayyu is a Rohingya, a stateless person. He has neither identity documents nor basic human rights. The everyday things that we do without a thought are forbidden for him: going out, taking a flight, working, studying, simply living.

In his country of Myanmar, his existence is not recognized and the very word 'Rohingya' is prohibited. Since 1982, when a law depriving the Rohingyas of citizenship was passed, this Muslim minority community has been subjected to absolute erasure. Their lands have been torched, villages razed to the ground, mosques destroyed, women and young girls raped and men killed to ensure that there is no trace left of them. According to the UN, successive waves of violence, cleansing operations and 'genocidal acts' had forced close to 740,000 people into neighbouring Bangladesh by August 2017.

Today, the approximately 600,000 Rohingyas who remain in Myanmar are cut off from the world. The climate has grown increasingly macabre and deleterious, ever since the one who orchestrated the 2017 massacres, General Min Aung Hlaing, seized power as the head of the country following a coup on 1 February 2021. Those like Mayyu, who fled to Bangladesh, have been reduced to a state of oblivion; caged like animals behind barbed wires, reliant on inconstant and insufficient – even non-existent – humanitarian aid.

It was at one of these refugee camps – the world's largest, in Kutupalong – that I met Mayyu in March 2018. The afternoon heat was suffocating that day. I waited for him, sheltered in an air-conditioned vehicle with tinted windows. When he slid into the back of the van, I immediately understood that he was different from the other refugees. I had a hard time believing that he had been living in that place for seven months. He exuded a rare elegance against such a backdrop; dressed in an immaculate and perfectly ironed white shirt, his ebony hair lightly slicked back. We were meeting to organize our work together over the next few weeks. I was in Bangladesh for the third time since the beginning of the crisis to report on women who became pregnant after rape. I had previously worked with several interpreters, but for a subject so delicate, I was looking for someone kind, respectful and capable of inspiring trust in people. I was immediately told about Mayyu, who was described to me as an adorable young man with a very large network, concerned about the fate of the women.

Right from the first interview we conducted together, it was clear that I had been told correctly. Mayyu's voice was low, attentive. He spoke calmly with the women, whom he considered to be his sisters or aunts, and didn't hesitate to ask me to stop my questions when the accounts were too painful. As we wandered the near-collapsing sandhills, he always walked in front of me; quick on his feet, with a parasol that protected him from the sun's rays. He was a real personality in the camps. He greeted everyone and took the time to exchange a few words with those who came to talk to him. Even so, he rarely opened up about himself. I sensed that he was overwhelmed by all the tragedies that he heard in his daily life as a translator and did not want to rush him.

One evening, while we were on the road, Mayyu handed me his phone and said, 'Look, these are my poems.' I was intrigued – it was the first time that I had met a poet within this community. 'We have been discriminated against for a long time. So as not to be considered a pariah, I wanted to become a poet and writer,' he told me. 'When I write down my feelings, I feel relieved. All my poems are dedicated to my people. I want to be their voice. I want us to get our rights back. I want to become a Rohingya author and be published internationally to carry the voice of my people all over the world.'

Two months after our first meeting, I went to the city of Maungdaw in Arakan, western Myanmar, where Mayyu was from. The region was off-limits for foreigners but a press trip organized by the Burmese government allowed me to visit. Everything Mayyu had told me was now in front of my eyes, all that he had endured. The spectacle was chilling, apocalyptic. The dense scent of burnt bodies floated in the air, as though life would never return to these streets again. I thought about the testimonies of the women we had met together, those who had told us how the Burmese soldiers had thrown their babies into fires. I felt sick.

Back in Paris, I couldn't stop thinking about Mayyu and his story. I was sure it would strike a chord with others too. Since 2013, I had interviewed scores of Rohingyas in Asia, Europe, Australia, the United States and more. I had published articles on crimes against humanity, mass rapes and human trafficking, always with the impression that the Rohingyas had been condemned to suffer the worst. Thanks to Mayyu, however, I finally had hope for his people. His passion was contagious; he was ready to do anything to save his people and never appeared disillusioned. He was prepared to fight against fate to help the Rohingyas regain their dignity.

I penned his portrait in *Le Figaro* under the title 'A poet at the heart of the genocide' with the idea of turning Mayyu's story into a book, because it deserved so much more. This little-known crisis, drowned in the torrential flow of news stories and very often forgotten by French newspapers, had to be experienced in the flesh to be understood. Mayyu was, to me, its best representative. He had experienced the worst, picked up the pieces and showed that behind every victim, there is a human being capable of taking destiny into their own hands – just like he did with his art.

During my last reporting assignment in Bangladesh in October 2019, I did not work with Mayyu in order to ensure his safety. Still, I could feel his presence. A number of young people had taken up poetry in the last few months after discovering his collections of poems. 'Mayyu Ali is the first poet of our generation to be known internationally. He has done so much for our community by encouraging the youth, including women, to pick up the pen. He is our hero,' cheered Zia, one of his apprentices.

Today, as a refugee in Canada, Mayyu is discovering what he has never known: freedom and security. But he remains an exception. Even as various NGOs publish an increasing number of alarming reports, crimes against the Rohingyas are still taking place. While we were finishing this book, activist Mohib Ullah – Mayyu's friend and mentor – was assassinated in Kutupalong. Since 2017, when the fifty-year-old family man fled to Bangladesh, Ullah had undertaken the painstaking task of collecting evidence to obtain recognition of the genocide of the Rohingyas. Despite the efforts of people like Ullah, the

International Criminal Court continues its investigation, and it might be years before justice is meted out.

This book is dedicated to all the Rohingyas who struggle day after day for their rights and the preservation of their heritage, and especially to my friend Omar Faruk, who died unexpectedly in May 2020. He was twenty-one years old. He dreamt of becoming a journalist and wanted to give a voice to those who had lost everything. He died in the place of his birth, in the biggest refugee camp in the world, not knowing what it is to be free. Like Mayyu, he had helped many reporters work effectively in the camps. Omar was one of the first people I spoke to about this project, and he had told me that he hoped to see the story of his people cross the borders. May he rest in peace.

For security reasons, several names have been changed. We use the term Rakhines to refer to the Buddhist population of Arakan, even though many French newspapers use the term Arakanais.

Emilie Lopes

2022

1

The earth orbits with two different worlds;
The hell and heaven
I left one, to discover other

– MAYYU ALI, 'A New Heaven'

I HAVE BEEN WAITING for this moment all my life. I have experienced the worst that man can do. The scent of death, the sound of bullets, the taste of erasure, the sight of blood flowing over the bodies of my brothers. Yes, I have only known the worst. That which imprisons and oppresses you; knocks you down and gnaws at you; crushes and grinds you. For a long time, I believed that I would know nothing more. Until one particular day in September 2021, when I opened the door to our new apartment in Toronto and watched my wife Shanas rush past me to explore its still-empty rooms. The wooden floor of our baby's future bedroom creaked beneath her footsteps and I followed with my daughter in my arms.

At that moment, seeing a smile light up Shanas's face, I realized that we were free. Free after so many years of oppression. The worst is far from me now, thousands of kilometres away; we are separated by several oceans and several continents. In Canada, I no longer risk anything. At last.

For the first time in my life, upon arriving in this country in August 2021, I felt inner peace. I no longer woke up with a start in the middle of the night because of my nightmares; I was no longer afraid that the police would come to arrest me. Instead, I breathed softly when asleep, not letting go of my wife's hand. I was happy; in pure, unadulterated bliss. I knew that my daughter would be safe; that my wife could go to university to finish her studies, take up a job and be recognized. We could finally envision a future, with the deep conviction that everything was going to be alright. I could sing and dance without fear – me, the shy guy. I could run for hours. I could do anything – after all, everything was possible now. I could finally live, when until then all I had done was survive.

And then the worst caught up with me yet again. All it took was a phone call. 'Mohib Ullah is dead. They killed him! They came into his office to murder him! They got him!' Mohib Ullah – my friend, my brother, my mentor, the one who taught me everything – was dead, killed by those who had long wanted *me* dead. The Arakan Rohingya Salvation Army (ARSA), an armed extremist group involved in the August 2017 attacks in Myanmar, which was now spreading terror in the camps of Bangladesh through abductions and assassinations.

Photos of my friend's body riddled with bullets began circulating online – I refused to look at them. His blood had stained the plastic rug where we used to spend days and nights together, thinking about the best strategy to have the genocide of our people recognized. Even when our friends would leave, the two of us would remain sitting on that mat, legs crossed, with our notebooks and telephones to verify the information we had. His wife would bring us a bowl of rice with lentils and a few pieces of dried fish. I would wait for him to start eating but he always gave me the biggest portion of protein with the words, 'Mayyu, we should be grateful for this meal. Thousands of our Rohingya brothers and sisters are on the roadsides and in the fields without food and shelter.' As he spoke, I would see tears running down his cheeks.

Mohib Ullah was no ordinary man. He was on a mission, willing to do anything to ensure that the world heard the voice of our people, the language of our brothers, the sound of our anger, the cries of our broken women. For two years, he knew that he was being targeted. Like me, he too had received death threats.

He had gone into hiding for some time, but had then returned to the camps, as though he had accepted the idea of dying for his struggle.

I left and he stayed. I survived and he is dead. Does that make any sense? Is this what it means to be a Rohingya? Must we suffer all our lives, even when we are free? Can we not have a little respite? I am free and my friend has been killed; my parents and brothers and sisters live in fear; my people are suffering. How does one come to terms with all this?

Since Ullah's death, I have come to know a new feeling, more pernicious than fear and much more powerful than anxiety: guilt. I am free, safe and alive, while my friends are being killed and my people are dying. How do I go on living? I am the only Rohingya survivor of the genocide who has been able to seek asylum in another country. Why only me? People are always astonished when I tell them that I have come from Bangladesh, because the Bangladeshi government has not issued exit permits to refugees since 2009. I am the first.

In Toronto, where I now live, I have discovered a new life. People are happy, they smile at each other and say hello. They are well dressed and smell good. Everything looks new, clean, in its right place, while I navigate between two worlds: the one where I come from and the other, where I will spend the rest of my life. Sometimes I do not know whether to laugh or cry.

I have an apartment in a large, well-maintained building. I have a small space where I write. The beds are soft, the furniture bright. I am discovering the comfort of modern life, something I have only seen in movies until now. We have a stove, a dishwasher and sliding drawers where we keep our plates and dishes. I come from a place which had no running water or electricity. I lived for years in a shelter made of tarpaulin and bamboo that was smaller than the bathroom of my new apartment. It seems almost unreal.

My neighbours are Canadian, African and Indian. They visit us every now and then and there is no fear or judgement on their part. Inayah, my seven-month-old daughter, loves rolling around the clean floor; she is full of laughter and happiness. I have bought two mugs with maple leaves drawn on them, the symbol of Canada – one for me and one for my wife. In the morning, when I prepare her coffee, Shanas calls me to our balcony's balustrade to admire the trees in the garden. 'This is a cup of freedom,' she says with relish. 'This coffee has such a unique flavour. I wish I could offer a taste of this to every Rohingya brother and sister.' This is how we start the day in our new home.

I have met many Rohingya people here, others who fled the violence in Myanmar over the years. Some know the history of our people only through the stories of their parents. The children go to good schools, the women work. They are all educated, cultured and their English is excellent. They are in good health and use their freedom wisely. These Rohingyas are socialized, privileged and intelligent because they have what my people never had: rights. Every time I meet them, I ask myself what it would be like if all my brothers and sisters enjoyed the same freedom. They could also have contributed to the betterment of society in Myanmar and in Bangladesh.

So why me? And why is something that was possible for me impossible for the others? I have been obsessed with these questions and though I do not have the answers, I know that I have a duty from hereon: to fight for my people until my last breath; for those who remain in Myanmar, for those who have taken refuge in Bangladesh, for those who escaped illegally and now live like slaves all over Asia. And to do this, I have to remember and tell my story – the story of my people and that of our genocide.

2

Even when I watch the sunrise,
I'm not living like you are
Without the fertility of hope I live,
Just like a sandcastle.

– MAYYU ALI, 'That's me, a Rohingya'

IN OUR CULTURE, WHEN a child is born, the midwife places the umbilical cord and placenta inside a large terracotta pot, the *hañri*. A member of the family, often the father or grandfather, then collects it to bury it. Once the pot is buried, like a plant, the organs take root. The child now belongs to the land – his native land, the eternal land. They are now one.

On this land, the child will take his first steps; he will grow and love. He will protect it. When he becomes a man, he in turn will bury a pot at the bottom of his garden when his children and grandchildren are born. And so, the story will continue. The man must die on this land and be buried close to the hañrí. This pot will be the mark of his birth, the proof of his existence. His essence. His purpose.

On 3 April 1991, my grandfather buried my pot in our yard. Much later, a few months before his death, he told me the story of my birth. 'There were no maternity wards in our district, so I went knocking on the door of the best traditional midwife in our village. Her name was Mostafani Maa. She was used to being woken up in the middle of the night for deliveries. After a long labour, she cried out that you were a boy. Before I could take you in my arms, she handed the hañrí over to me. I went out, knelt down, took the earth in my hands. It was an accomplishment.'

I listened to him, trying to hide my tears. His voice trembled. And when he asked, I promised him that I would, throughout my life, defend the honour of belonging to this country that was his, mine and of our ancestors. I had to leave our land to understand the meaning of these words; to write my memoir and honour this promise. To ward off our fate as the wretched of the earth and revive the colours tarnished by war.

When I remember the little boy I once was, I see a stranger who haunts my nostalgic reveries. It is as though happiness existed in fragments. I remember eagerly awaiting the arrival of summer, when fields were bare and the farmers had finished harvesting their crops. The joy of running barefoot on the barely tilled earth. My heart racing, temples pounding, the first droplets of sweat on my forehead … and the infinite horizon in front of me, without any borders.

I would race to go faster than my friend Johar, while our third playmate Aung Naing tried to catch me or distract me with his cries: 'I'm coming, I'm going to get you!' Nothing could take the wind out of our sails. Our races would always end with a dive into the Purma river. Whoever came in first was declared champion of the day. I would jump as high as I could to be able to touch the slimy shallows. Holding my breath, in the depths of the water, all I could hear was my heartbeat. I would close my eyes to make the pleasure last, delighted by the thought that when I came back to the surface, my friends would be beaming at me.

I loved the purity of the landscapes of my childhood. The sky would merge with the verdant Mayu mountains in the distance, to the east of my village Boli Bazar. At daybreak, a thick mist would rise from the summits. An hour or two later, the first rays of sunlight would appear. Once the view cleared, the plains appeared – the green and ochre of the fields, dotted with the shadows of grazing cows. From dawn till dusk, without respite, the farmers sowed and harvested potatoes, aubergines, peppers and onions. Umbrellas protected them from the heat, *zuirs* from hailstones. Nothing changed, come rain or shine.

My neighbourhood ran along the Purma river which, further south, joined the Naf river that marked the border with Bangladesh. During the sweltering summer evenings, my parents, siblings and I would sit on the riverbank to enjoy the cool breeze on our skin. We watched the sun disappear across the riverside, taking the tumult of the day with it.

The Purma was sacred. It fed the entire village with fish, true gifts from God. To not offend it, our huts were built alongside the watercourse. But during the rainy season, the current created waves which crashed violently on the shore, destroying dozens of shacks and the lives of families who were forced to relocate. Like in this poem which my grandfather used to recite:

'The rain out there,
The roaring sound of the waves,
The demon in the Purma stream,
Destroys everything along the shore.'

It is in this river that I have my best memories. Johar, Aung Naing and I loved slipping inside the old boats that slumbered on the banks to play at being great navigators.

We could 'sail' for hours on end. Johar, the leader of our gang, was the captain and Aung Naing and I were sailors. It was quite a sight: three boys paddling around, sandals held between our fingertips and shirts wet from the water that splashed every time we moved.

When I wasn't at the river I liked making toys, like cars out of plastic bottles, rubber and bamboo. Usually, around sunset, Aung Naing would call me for a game of *chinlon* in the fields. Four or five of us would stand in a semi-circle, passing around a ball of woven bamboo. We had to make sure the ball didn't touch the ground using our chests, legs and heads but never our hands. Aung Naing, short and stocky, was very good at the game.

Our afternoons looked like this: children enjoying games and jokes. There were these moments of fleeting happiness, but we were constantly under surveillance. I became aware of this feeling for the first time when I was four years old. I was playing with my friends in the alleyway in front of my house. Suddenly, a convoy of soldiers appeared on the road. They were coming towards us. As soon as I saw them, I ran to hide in my neighbour's garden. I was shaking. My heart was beating really fast

From my hiding place among the interlaced bamboo, I saw the grim face of a man. He was wearing black boots that went up to his knees and his steps, heavy, resembled those of a racehorse. Small bags hung from the belt of his dark green pants and he held a long pistol. Behind him, dozens of men had their hands tied together with a lengthy rope. Some were stripped to their waist, others had weights on their shoulders. I couldn't clearly distinguish what they were – these thin figures, their ribs jutting out. The soldiers were watching them, forcing them forward. I had never seen anything like this before in my village.

Just ten minutes later, the group was gone. My heart was beating even faster. The road was empty now; the sounds of my friends playing had disappeared. Night had fallen. When I reached home, still reeling in shock, I could barely bring myself to speak. My father interrupted our conversation with a reassurance that the men would not return to our village. 'Please give him a bath,' he said to my mother. The cold water from the pump in the garden, which served as a shower, felt good. After dinner, my mother lay down next to me on the floor mat and lulled me to sleep.

Whenever I think of my childhood, I still feel that distant fear – fear that can crop up anywhere, at any moment. Like a sandcastle – beautiful but pitiful, without hope or a foundation – buried by the sea and the kick of a boot.

3

Kings in colours
Their kingdom so eminent
Mosques and temples together,
Tigers and goat drank from the same pond.

– MAYYU ALI, 'The Shared Kingdom'

I WAS BORN A Rohingya, like all my ancestors who walked our homeland. This word defines my religion and ethnicity, where I belong and what I ultimately am. It also condemns me to be a child without a birth certificate, a man without citizenship, a human being without rights. Myanmar has crossed out our existence from its history – obscured it, erased it. My life is worth nothing in their eyes. I am a maggot that spoils their fruit, cancer eating away at their organs. A foreigner who, as they put it, has 'invaded' their lands. A pariah, a damned one, a nonentity, subhuman.

Our lives changed with the arrival of the dictator Ne

Win, who seized power after a coup d'état in 1962. He wanted to lead a cultural revolution and the majority ethnic group of Myanmar (then Burma) – the Barmars, who were Burmese-speaking Buddhists – became his point of reference. Win intended to 'Barmarize' the country, though we Muslims represented 4 per cent of the population and were already marginalized like so many other minorities. In 1964, Win's decision to cancel a programme in the Rohingya dialect on the national radio was a sign of things to come.

The violence began in 1978. Operation Nagamin, also known as 'Dragon King', was carried out in northern Arakan, aimed at taking a census of citizens and throwing out foreigners. Mass murder, rape and destruction of mosques ravaged the state and over 200,000 Rohingyas fled to Bangladesh seeking refuge. That year marked the beginning of our genocide. It was then etched into our national history by the 1982 Citizenship Act. The act excluded Rohingyas from the 135 recognized ethnic groups of Burma, making us the largest community of stateless people in the world. We were Bengalis in their eyes, foreigners who came illegally from Bangladesh under British rule in the nineteenth century, undeserving of basic rights.

A year after my birth, in 1992, the junta established the Nasaka, a security force meant to combat illegal immigration. It was mainly comprised of border guards. Thereupon, they refused to register Muslim newborns, which meant I never received my birth certificate.

Yet, before all this, we were at peace in Myanmar. My grandfather, Ali Akbar, often told me so. Every evening, after dinner, we had a ritual. He would take me to my room and sit on the floor. I would rest my head on his legs, covered by his zubba, a traditional attire worn by Muslim men. Long-sleeved, it covers the entire body, from arm to ankle. His deep, monotonous voice soothed me; his warm breath brushed my face. From my position I could see every detail of his face. His half-moon-like eyes, the furrows beneath them, the sagging skin of his eyelids. I loved to grab his big, white beard and touch his large hands. His skin was so thin that I could feel his knuckles.

As he stroked my hair, my grandfather would tell me the stories of his life, and our ancestors. 'A long time ago, in the fourteenth century, we had a kingdom whose capital was Pattor Qilla (Mrauk-U). At that time, the kings of Arakan were Muslims: Shikandar Shah, Jalalal Shah, Salim Shah, Sultan Shah. The capital was built by Muslims and Buddhists together. The city is an eternal symbol of our unity. The kingdom flourished for centuries along the Bay of Bengal because of trade. We were very prosperous. At that time, there were only natural borders.'

This was the first time that I heard the word 'Buddhist'. 'They are the Rakhines who live to the north of our village,' he told me. 'The only difference between them and the Rohingyas is religion.' My grandfather always punctuated his stories with advice that I would only understand much later. 'The Hindus and Rakhines of the village are our friends. Do not forget that. You are here in your country, on your land. Don't let anyone tell you otherwise.'

My grandfather was a local personality, and the house was always full of people who wanted to give their regards and seek his counsel. Now that he had explained the differences between our communities to me, I had fun identifying Buddhists and Hindus, even Rohingyas. From a child's perspective, I noticed that we had darker skin than the Buddhists, who closely resembled the Chinese. Their noses were straight, while mine was flat; their eyebrows were thin and mine were thick. As for the Hindus, they had the same skin colour as us but their women wore long, red veils.

These differences didn't matter to me. In my village, pagodas stood alongside mosques and monks mixed with imams. Still, each community had its own neighbourhood. We lived to the east, in a group of twenty-odd houses huddled together in front of the river.

The house my parents moved into after their wedding had six rooms while other houses in the area often only had one, where all the members of a family crammed together. The walls were made of bamboo, the floor of beaten earth and the roof was covered with thatch that my father and grandfather replaced after the rainy season. The wooden veranda at the front of the house was protected by an enormous jackfruit tree. In summer, the temperature could rise close to 45 degrees celsius.

From our veranda one could see the mosque, the oldest in the district of Maungdaw. It was built in 1823 by the Bolis, a well-known Rohingya family. I went there every Friday for prayers. There were always men who stayed back afterwards, chatting under a tree and putting the world to rights. Sometimes I joined them but said nothing. I simply liked to listen to the elders speak.

Further up the river stood the Hindu neighbourhood, in front of which the Nasaka post monitored the city and its comings and goings. A little further north lived the Buddhists, right next to the high school and central pagoda. The climate of terror was intensifying for us. The law was becoming stricter. Police searches, inspections, arbitrary taxation, requisitions – everything was permitted.

The marketplace, at the heart of the village, was the meeting ground for all communities. The Buddhists were known to be good goldsmiths and the Hindus, skilled hairdressers. Many Rohingyas sold their crops on the dusty ground, protected by plastic tarpaulins. My mother sold vegetables from my grandfather's fields while my father sold the fish he caught. Customers haggled over the prices but my mother never gave in. Nearby, some women fried samosas in frying pans held over hot embers by bricks. I loved these potato and rice fritters and devoured while they were still sizzling, so much so that I had to keep my mouth open to not burn myself. Once I bit into the fried crust, the batter would melt into my mouth ... it was divine.

I was born in Arakan, one of the poorest regions of the country. In fact, it is one of the most isolated areas in the world, separated from the rest of Myanmar by a mountain range. The neglected rural state had no electricity or drinking water at the time; no public infrastructure except a few hospitals in the main towns, a handful of schools and a university in its capital city Sittwe. The bumpy dirt roads made it difficult to reach the villages, and some were completely cut off from the rest of the Arakan.

The local people sustained themselves with fishing

and agriculture. Most of them had such little means that they sent their children to labour in the fields. My maternal grandfather owned some land, which allowed him to provide an education to his children. As for my father, he came from a very poor family of fishermen who were not educated and so he never learnt to read. After his father died when he was only ten, he became the head of the family and had to take responsibility for his many brothers and sisters.

My father Amir Ali used to wrestle and before his marriage, he won a gold medal at a tournament held in Maungdaw. He had a wrestler's physique: short, lean and sturdy. His scalp had already started to thin when I was young, and he was a man of few words. My mother Khaleda Khatun was beautiful and much taller than him. She had dark eyes, and a mole embellished her left eyelid. Strands of ebony hair always fell on her face, though she tried to tuck them under her veil.

The village school was located close to the market. I would walk there with my brother Sabar Ali, three years my senior. Every morning, before leaving, he would apply coconut oil to tame his frizzy hair. I still remember him hiding in the bedroom, brushing his hair back in front of a chipped mirror.

Ever since I was little, I had wanted to go to school and learn to read like my brother. Every evening, I would see him buried in his notebooks or reciting lessons to our mother. They communicated in Burmese, the language of the school. I didn't understand it then – I only knew our Rohingya language. The day before school started, my brother advised me to pay close attention. The teachers' pronunciation would differ from ours, he said. They were Rakhines and had their own dialect. Everyone spoke Burmese, the official language, at school but with different accents.

On my first day of school, at the age of five, I was proud to wear the official uniform. A white shirt and a green longyi, a piece of fabric that is tied at the waist and resembles a skirt. My grandfather gifted me a shoulder bag which I used to carry my few books. The school was made up of five wooden buildings, housing students from nursery to high school. At its centre was a large courtyard lined with trees, in which the flag of Myanmar fluttered. Students were always running across the complex in every direction.

The classroom, with its crumbling walls, was basic, with a low table in the centre and a board. There was a wooden chair for the teacher. We had to sit with our legs curled back on floorboards, which creaked under our footsteps. My mother had explained to me that it was forbidden in the Burmese tradition to stretch out one's legs once seated, as it was considered a sign of disrespect.

The teacher was a Buddhist, just like my brother had told me. I noticed her accent immediately – she spoke like the Rakhine people. She began writing letters of the Burmese alphabet on the board with chalk – *kagyi* and *kakway* – and taught us how to pronounce them. I was completely lost. The other Rohingya students and I looked at each other, puzzled.

At noon, the bell rang. Everyone stood up and placed their hands on their chests. It was time to sing 'Kaba Ma Kyei', the national anthem. My brother had told me to expect this. I knew the words by heart and attempted to recite them as loudly as possible. I felt my vocal chords vibrating in my throat as I tried to honour my country.

... as the world exists, we love Myanmar, the true heritage of our ancestors.
We shall safeguard the Union by sacrificing our lives.
This is our Nation, our motherland and our own land.
Let us serve unitedly for the interest of our Nation, our motherland.
That is our duty for the precious land.

I spent the rest of my school years amongst Rakhines, Rohingyas and Hindus. We sat on the same benches and wore the same uniforms. We played together, drank the same water, ate the same meals and helped each other with homework. We were too young to know what it meant to fear those unlike us or view each other as threats. I couldn't care less about my peers' religions or our differences. Does a child concern himself with the skin colour of his classmates?

4

Fear is my first feeling
When I open my eyes in morning
Just life in empty joy
Sound sleep through the lonesome dark

– MAYYU ALI, 'The Nasaka and a Rohingya'

I SHARED MY ROOM with my brother and younger sister. We slept on floormats and my mother had sewn pillows for us using straw and old rags for a little more comfort. Sabar liked to tell us scary stories which often woke our sister Sonia with a start. But there was one night that her screams did not make us laugh one bit. Our father rushed into the room, frightened, as if he had seen a ghost. 'Get out of this room quick and come to the living room!' he ordered.

My mother and grandfather were already standing in the middle of the room, surrounded by five men in uniform whom I had never seen before. They were searching our house. They left nothing untouched, emptying drawers and opening the doors to our bedrooms. Sonia burst into tears. My mother held my sister in her arms but that didn't help, she continued to sob. My father handed our family record book to one of the men, and we obeyed when he ordered us to sit individually.

'Who is the head of the family?' demanded one of his colleagues, seemingly hesitating between my father and grandfather.

'That will be me, Amir Ali,' was my father's curt reply.

The man called out our names one by one. First my grandfather's, Ali Akbar, who stared straight into his eyes in silent defiance. Petrified, my mother kept her head lowered, only letting out a sound to signify her presence. Next, it was my turn. I was afraid that I would be incapable of answering. Then it was Sonia. But my older brother Azim was missing, which intrigued the officer. My father stood up with folded hands, a sign of respect, and explained that my brother was a teacher who worked in a distant village and no longer slept at our house.

After consulting with their colleagues, the men decided to leave. I could hear their boots thumping on the floor of our veranda. Dogs were barking outside. They went from house to house sowing the seeds of fear. Gradually. Unexpectedly. That was the first of many other – seemingly endless – nights of terror. I was never able to sleep peacefully again.

The following day, Johar told me during recess that his family had experienced the same thing. He was a Rohingya like me and we had been friends since nursery school. Good-natured, jovial and sardonic, he was always able to make me laugh. But lately I could barely recognize him. His eyes had lost their sparkle. Normally a gourmand, he no longer touched his meals. That same fear had settled into his heart.

'Do you think that they are doing this to everyone?' Johar wondered anxiously. 'My father tells me that we are being targeted because we are Muslims.' I had never pondered this question. I decided to check with Aung Naing, my closest Buddhist friend. We sat in the same row and studied together when we weren't at the river with Johar. When I asked if the Nasaka had come to his house as well, Aung Naing told me that they had been spared. I did not want to believe it. I could feel my world changing.

One morning, a few days later, a new guard came looking for my father. 'Tell your father that he has been summoned to the police station,' he instructed. 'He owes us money.' Rohingya fishermen had to pay a sum of 50,000 kyats a year to obtain fishing permits, which amounted to two and a half months of my father's salary. Otherwise, they were arrested. That very evening, as I reported the incident to my father, there was a question

I was dying to ask. Were the Rakhines forced to pay as well? The answer, of course, was no. But my father did not want me to know more and got up from the table.

Things were slowly becoming clear to me now. At seven years old I understood that my life was going to be different in all aspects, from birth to marriage. Rohingyas were no longer allowed to have more than two children. Before getting married, engaged couples had to go to the Nasaka post to validate their marriage and pay a sum of 100,000 kyats. Here, too, the conditions were stringent. The bride could not wear a veil and the groom had to be clean-shaven, which was an insult to our religion. We were being persecuted, made to erase all that was distinctive about us

One of my older sisters Sofia was set to marry a mullah. My parents insisted they ask for permission; they were afraid that their daughter would be arrested. They had heard numerous stories in the neighbourhood of Rohingya couples being abducted or imprisoned for years. My mother was worried sick – she couldn't imagine a ceremony that would land her daughter behind bars. But Sofia's future husband wouldn't have it. To him, it was out of the question to shave his beard or abide by rules that he felt were unfair. They got married in 1998 against my parents' wishes and without authorization. When my father found out, he asked Sofia to flee Myanmar. She has since been living in Bangladesh with her husband and children. They were never able to come back to see us. I was deprived of my sister for years because of a slip of paper and a beard that was too long.

Very soon, we were forced to be apart from my older brother Azim as well. He was the only one in our family who had earned a higher secondary certificate, the first to become a teacher. It was such an honour for us, especially for my father who could proudly say that his son was teaching children to read and write. I saw very little of him since he travelled all over Arakan for work, but I wanted to follow his example. Azim was my role model, always in tune with fashion trends, wearing the trendiest T-shirts and longyi.

In 2005, he decided to build a house not far from our village for his wife and two children. One evening, he didn't come back home. Everyone was worried. I knew immediately that he must have been arrested. The next morning, I rushed to the Nasaka police station. Azim was lying down in a dark and gloomy room that smelled of piss and vomit. The stench made me nauseous. He was tied up and wasn't allowed to speak to me. His left temple was bloodied – he had been beaten. My brother, my mentor, so full of fortitude, looked like dying prey caught in a net.

To my panicked questions the guards only smirked

and gave no answers. Eventually one of them raised his fist at me and I was forced to leave. After five days, and a payment of 500,000 kyats, Azim was released. He was made to sign a paper stating that he had not been interrogated by the Nasaka, otherwise he would've remained in prison. He had faced such severe punishment for not applying for a building permit for his house. In 2008, after much intimidation, Azim decided to leave Myanmar. I have not seen my brother since.

5

Shouldn't we look back at our shared kingdom ?
Let's rebuild the bridge together.
A new peaceful future like our past waiting for us.
We have nothing to pain more but much to gain.

– MAYYU ALI, 'The Shared Kingdom'

IN MY BROTHER'S ABSENCE, I rediscovered a brotherly bond with Aung Naing, my childhood friend. In high school, we spent our days together, always sitting side by side in class. We shared our meals and studied together in the library. He had delicate features, and a prominent jawline which was accentuated by his shaven head. He always wore crisp, perfectly ironed white shirts. Like me, he was the youngest son of his parents. His father was a well-known goldsmith who worked with Rohingyas in the market. The only thing that set us apart was religion. But none of that mattered to us.

We often studied at my house after school. My mother

would cook luri fira for us, a Rohingya snack made with fried rice and spicy dried beef. We would sit under the shade of the old mango tree in our garden – its trunk was very thick and I enjoyed peeling off strips of its bark. In springtime, mangoes fell from the tree. There would be dozens on the ground and I could eat them all. I absolutely loved them. I would split a mango open with my hands and sink my teeth into the overripe orange flesh; its juice would drip down my chin, onto my shirt and sometimes even my sandals.

I used to go to his house too. The first time was an overwhelming experience. I'd never been to a Buddhist neighbourhood before. There were around a dozen single-storey houses in his community. Like ours, their walls were made of bamboo and the roofs were covered with thatch. But none of them had the fencing that surrounded our houses, *zowlee*. In the kitchen, his mother was preparing a traditional Burmese paste made from dried fish and shrimp. I had never tasted it before. It smelled so strongly of sour and fermented ingredients that I had to cover my nose with my hand; it was insufferable.

Aung Naing saw the look of disgust on my face and smiled. Behind the house, there was a yard with five pigs stuffing themselves with rice mixed in dirty water. I wondered how one could eat these poor creatures who bathed in filth. The smell of the pigs was even worse than the soup. Aung Naing paid no heed and invited me into his home. Inside, I noticed coloured posters and golden statuettes of the Buddha. His mother was small but very strong and like many Buddhists, she had applied *thanaka* on her cheeks, a paste that protects the skin from the sun. Unveiled, her hair was tied at her nape.

I used to spend hours at Aung Naing's house. I was comfortable and never felt fearful or tense in any way. We didn't talk about religion. In school, we had grown so close that we could now understand each other's language and culture.

My happiest memory from this period remains the moment when the results of our higher secondary examinations were declared. Like every morning, my father had his breakfast outside. He liked meeting his friends at the local inn after *fajr*, the first prayer of the day. He often said that it was his favourite ritual.

The day before the results, there had been a storm and a few drops of rain had fallen through the roof. The wind was blowing; I couldn't sleep, impatient. That morning, 20 June 2008, my father came home earlier than usual. I had already said my prayers and recited verses from the Qur'an. He had just met one of my teachers and hurried back to tell me that I had passed my higher secondary exams.

Education was of supreme importance in our family. My grandfather sacrificed a cow for me, just like he had promised when I was very little. This was our custom during major events. All my friends were present in our garden: Aung Naing, Johar and more. It was our first meeting after the exams, and Aung Naing gifted me a Burmese novel. My father prepared rice and potatoes with the sacrificed meat. He was used to cooking for large gatherings and people often invited him to cook for weddings.

I enjoyed the respite, looking carefully at each and every person present. I wanted to capture the moment. Savour it. Smartphones didn't exist back then, nor did selfies. We only had our minds to hold onto these memories. That day was one of the happiest of my life.

Things took a turn for the worse that same year. I was seventeen years old and for some time now, I'd been feeling a sense of unease grow inside our house – a palpable but inexpressible anxiety. Our gestures were becoming lifeless; our exchanges brief, trite. We stayed out of each other's way. It made me sad. Grandfather hardly spoke anymore. He stayed in his garden and seemingly just stared at his flowers. No one dared to disturb him – not even me, his favourite grandson. His back was bent, as though he was carrying a grief that grew heavier with each passing day. For several weeks, he barely ate, slept poorly and appeared to be lost.

Then, one afternoon, I overheard that an order had been issued to seize the land of the Rohingyas of our village. My mother was worried. She wondered what was going to become of us without the harvest. Were we going to starve to death?

By the end of September 2008, my grandfather's land had been confiscated by the district administration. He had owned more than ten hectares, bequeathed to him by his father, and suddenly he was left with nothing. I could see how the experience debilitated my grandfather. He exhausted himself going to the District Commissioner's office to show his property papers, only to be told by the commissioner that it was an order by the Burmese government.

For the first time in my life, I saw my grandfather break down. 'The land is gone. It's over. My heart is gone. My life is over.' He could no longer hold back his tears. I could not understand what was going on. How could the land, his land, be taken away? I called out to him but to no avail. Usually very energetic and enthusiastic, my grandfather was on a different plane altogether. His land was his life. His dignity. His existence. Without his land, he did not exist.

Overnight, bulldozers replaced the farmers in our fields. These machines swallowed up the entire lives of people, dug out our grains and our crops. The pots of my ancestors were destroyed, vestiges of so many past lives. Our own land had become the burial ground of our culture. A few days later, houses on stilts sprouted from the ground with tin roofs that no one in the village could afford. New wooden houses – clean, lifeless, untethered from all things past.

Whole families of strangers began arriving in the area. They wore dirty shirts that were too big for them and looked even poorer than the people in our village. Yellowish circles were drawn on their cheeks with thanaka. They had come from the southern regions of Myanmar to repopulate our lands. With our existence denied, the government wanted to create a new world made up of people that looked like the junta's leaders: light-skinned Buddhists with slanted eyes and thin noses. Everything we were not. To achieve this dream we had to be erased, wiped out from history. Every trace of our existence had to be washed out, once again.

After 1992, the government escalated the creation of these 'model villages', which were called NaTaLa. The policy consisted of confiscating our lands in northern Arakan and repopulating them. It is difficult to obtain accurate figures because access to this region is so arduous, but Amnesty International counted twenty-six model villages in 2004. Houses and other facilities such as schools were often constructed during the campaigns, forcing Rohingyas into hard labour. The stolen lands were also used to expand military bases and camps. What was going to happen next?

My grandfather was forced to sell his entire herd, leaving him with almost nothing. He was ninety-six years old when he died. The day before his death, lying weakly on a mat, he tried to express his last wishes. He had kept an ox and wanted us to continue feeding it. After his death, we would have to sacrifice it and organize a traditional funeral ceremony, with the Buddhists and Hindus of the village in attendance. Then my grandfather took my hands and asked me to keep all our identity documents and property deeds in a safe place. 'Do not lose any document. You will need them to prove that this is our home and that this land belongs to us.'

Forty days after his death, my uncle killed an ox. We invited all our neighbours: Hindus, Buddhists, my grandfather's friends and local religious leaders. After lunch, the imam of the mosque prayed for the soul of the deceased as is our tradition. We were all gathered together. This was one of the last times.

6

Even when I breathe the sky's air
I'm not human like you are.

– MAYYU ALI, 'That's me, a Rohingya'

GRANDFATHER'S DEATH HAD THE impact of a tsunami on the entire family. Shortly after his passing, Aung Naing came to visit me. This was usual but that day, there was a lull in the garden. The grass had become overgrown and dense rose bushes covered the path. He was sad for me; he too missed my grandfather, who was always around and would often break into our conversations. There was something worrisome about his demeanour. He wanted to tell me something important, even though he knew that it wasn't the right time. I tried to make a guess at what he was holding back but truth be told, I had absolutely no idea. It took him a few minutes to admit that he would be going away to the university at the beginning of the new academic year.

I felt like my heart was about to explode. Attending university was my dream as well, and that of my grandfather. But without him and his land, how could we possibly pay the tuition fee? That very evening my father promised to call my older brother. He had been living in Saudi Arabia since he left Myanmar and could help send the required money.

This glimpse of hope was short-lived. I needed an identity card to go to university but I didn't have one, since I was not recognized as a Burmese citizen. The only ID I could apply for was a temporary white card, which would register me as a Bengali. It was a denial of our history and more importantly, it rendered me a stranger in my own country. Without this card, no Rohingya – not even a student – had been allowed to move from one village to another since the establishment of the Nasaka.

Johar and I travelled to downtown Maungdaw to complete the necessary formalities. Since there was no public transportation, old jeeps made the trip from the village on bumpy roads twice a day. The car bobbed and bounced like a frog over every pothole. There were twelve of us crammed onto the dilapidated seats, including two Buddhist women. After three hours on the road, the driver asked us to get off – we had reached the first checkpoint. The Nasaka monitored every entry into and exit from the village. Once I got out of the car, I handed a border guard my student ID card.

To my shock, the man started yelling. I had never seen so much anger in someone's eyes. Tiny red dots pierced through his eyes as if they were about to explode in front of me. 'Get down, all you Bengalis!' shouted someone with a Burmese accent. I couldn't believe it. It was the first time I'd heard someone saying that word out loud. It was an insult to our history.

'Go to the checkpoint!' the guard in front of me ordered, pointing his gun. He was chewing a betel nut and kept squirting its red juice from between his teeth. I felt nauseous. All the Rohingyas got out of the car for an inspection, but the two Buddhist ladies were spared.

Before we could make sense of the situation, the guards let us pass in exchange for 500 kyats. The car continued its journey. No one dared to speak anymore. The word 'Bengali' still echoed in my ears. Why were the Rohingyas made to get out of the car for an inspection? What was this differentiation? Why did we have to pay again? Why? I wanted to bang my head against the window, helpless in the face of such injustice.

Once we reached our destination, we went directly to the district immigration office with our documents. It was a large building made of corrugated iron, guarded by armed men, with the Burmese flag flying overhead. The officer in charge of the files was out of town. We would have to come back another day.

A few weeks later, we received our much talked-about temporary white cards. This precious open sesame had come at a cost of 19,500 kyats each. Fortunately, my brother was able to send me the money to pay for these expenses. The inspections, threats and insults mattered little to us now – we were finally going to university. I would use this opportunity to equip myself to one day ensure that my rights were recognized.

Johar and I couldn't stop jumping for joy. The time had come to enrol at the university, so we made an appointment with the court clerk in charge of our files. Even this simple step did not go smoothly. 'Your file has been rejected,' the clerk informed me in a dry, detached voice at our meeting. 'Your name in the census book does not match the one in your school records.' It was pretty common at the time for immigration officers to spell our names differently in family censuses. The clerk added in the same tone that I needed another recommendation from the village administrator to resolve the problem. Meanwhile, Johar's file had been accepted.

I obtained a new recommendation a few days later for a fee of 2,000 kyats. Despite all the hurdles, I was finally going to be able to get a college education. That very evening, my older sister organized a dinner at her place to celebrate. During our conversation, she offered me money. I rarely saw my sister, since she was so much older than me. This gift from her moved me deeply. 'You'll need this in Sittwe,' she said. 'Study. Follow your dreams. Grandpa would've been happy and proud of you.'

All the students in our village decided to leave for Sittwe together on 26 December. Everything was packed and ready in my room. I had bought a backpack to carry my books and belongings. A few days before the planned date, a man from the village came to my house early in the morning to tell us that there was a call for my father from Saudi Arabia. At the time, we had to travel to the north of the village to use the only satellite phone available to call overseas. Standing in front of the receiver, I watched my father's face shatter. He was livid.

The caller was a friend of my brother's, who wanted to let us know that he had been arrested by the Saudi police due to visa issues. My father was in shock; tears rolled down his face. This was the worst moment of our lives. We had just lost my grandfather. My brother was in prison. We had no land left. Aung Naing, Johar and all my other friends were prepared to go off to the university. And without my brother's financial support, my university dreams were shattered. I was left alone, devastated, unable to do anything.

I had to wait two whole years to see my friends again. In the summer of 2010, they gave me the most wonderful surprise. I was in the garden when I saw Johar arrive, looking as though he had never left. I pinched myself; I couldn't believe my eyes. He hugged me tight – almost choking me – and then said that Aung Naing hadn't been able to come. I was disappointed. Aung Naing was like a brother to me, the one I'd shared everything with since we were children. Little did I know that he was crouched behind the kitchen door. 'Stupid as always!' Johar laughed. 'Of course he's here.'

Aung Naing came out of hiding. He hadn't changed one bit. He wore a familiar longyi and shirt. The three of us were finally reunited under the shade of the mango tree, just like before. It was very hot, so we rushed inside to sit on the plastic chairs that grandpa used to reserve for his guests. My father wasn't at home. He was out fishing in the creek. I brought a pot of drinking water and cups for my friends. Johar twirled his hair with his fingers. It had grown longer, with a beard to match, and his face had thickened.

According to them, the university campus was gigantic. 'The buildings are so big. The courtyard is endless,' Aung Naing described. They talked about the beautiful beaches; the big cinema hall in the city centre; the beautiful girls in their class!

The following day, Aung Naing came back alone. He wanted to speak to me. He offered me a piece of paper – a teacher recruitment advertisement from the district education office. The deadline was in a few days. Aung Naing and I decided to apply, to fulfil our childhood dream. All we needed was a high school diploma and I thought we stood a good chance of succeeding.

As with all administrative documents, we had to make the trip to Maungdaw in an old Jeep. But this time, I had my white card with me. When the car stopped at a checkpoint a few kilometres in, a Nasaka officer came towards us and started shouting. All the Rohingyas were made to get off, one after the other. I looked at Aung Naing – I didn't want to get down. When the man got in the car to check our bags and luggage, he saw me and ordered me to get out. I was frightened. Aung Naing followed me. I tried to explain to the guard that we were friends who had grown up together; that we were travelling to apply to become teachers. In response, the officer spat, 'You are a *kalar*. He is a *thai yen thar*. You are not from here.'

Kalar. Bengali. Bengali. Kalar. What did these words mean? Who had invented them? Why? *Why*? 'Kalar' means 'illegal immigrant' in Burmese. It is a racial slur used by the armed forces, the worst of its kind. On the other hand, 'thai yen thar' refers to Buddhists, meaning that they are indigenous to Myanmar. Aung Naing and I were friends. We were born in the same year, in the same village. We had studied in the same school and shared the same dream. How had he become a thai yen thar, while I was a kalar? Why did I have to get out of the car and not him?

When we finally arrived at the district education office, Aung Naing told the official, 'We have come to apply for the teaching posts.' I said the same thing with a Rakhine accent so that he wouldn't guess my identity. The man gave me a knowing smirk and I felt humiliated. Once again.

A few weeks later, Aung Naing was selected and I was rejected. I was born to Rohingya parents. He was born to Buddhist parents. This was the only difference that mattered now in my country, and the realization made me feel inferior. We had the same degree, the same skills, but I had the wrong religion. Enduring such experiences year after year, I discovered a world where two friends cannot sit together in a car. A world where facial features, skin colour and religion are reasons for discrimination.

Fear had become a common occurrence in our daily lives, eating away at us from the inside. This was the government's ploy in the insidious war that they had decided to wage against us. We had nothing left; they were taking everything from us. The first signs of the anti-Muslim pogrom and the shadow of Buddhist ultra-nationalism were already manifesting, two years before the outbreaks of intercommunal violence between the Rakhines and Rohingyas in our state in 2012.

7

Knowledge is candle
Lightening your life,
Brightening your brain
And…
Shining your future.

– MAYYU ALI, 'Success'

I WAS SHATTERED, DEVASTATED by the hatred. It was suffocating me. Every attempt to change my path was blocked out by a shadow – of my history – that prevented any progress. Those in power were deciding what I should do, or rather what I was forbidden from doing: travelling, studying, learning. They had created a world in which the only right I had was to exist, like I was doomed.

In those days, my mouth always felt dry and my saliva, thick with the bitter taste of injustice. I found myself returning to the same question on a loop: What crime are we guilty of? I had become a timid and fearful young man given to nostalgia, not the type to step out of line. I was caught in a vice, between sorrow and anger; dejection and rage; the urge to yell out in distress and the fear of speaking out too loudly or crossing the line. My voice remained quiet, I kept a low profile and became docile.

Every evening, in my bedroom, I would put this duality that was eating away at me down on paper. I muttered the words aloud before sketching out my pain – my desire to break away from this life that had already been mapped out for me. I wrote everything in a notebook that I hid out of timidity. I would slide my notebook behind the cover of a book, then bend my back and keep close to the pages as I wrote, as though to keep every alphabet intact, for fear of being caught. Often, my mother would come into my bedroom and I would reassure her that I was studying when she urged me not to stay up late.

In the light shining from the *sarag,* a kerosene lamp that burned as the night wore on, I would spend hours writing. When I finished, my eyes would be reddened by the fumes. It was the only moment when I felt truly alive. Writing wasn't a vocation – it was the only solution that I'd found for my disturbed psyche, like a shield that protected me. It was instinctive. I no longer felt compelled to brood and mope around. Every word that I put to paper lifted a weight off my shoulders.

I could not share my passion with those close to me. My family were fishermen, farmers, people of the soil. Art had never figured in our conversations. I had never heard of any Rohingya writer or poet. Nevertheless, writing became a part of my daily existence.

One afternoon, I decided to visit my friend Shafiul Hoque. He lived just a stone's throw away from my house. We often got together to talk about changing the world and dream of other places – two teenagers caught in a trap trying to find a way out. Shafiul had passed his higher secondary exam the same year I did and he too wandered about aimlessly because he could not go to university. His parents, poor like mine, could not afford to pay for his education. We usually liked to chat outside under the shade of the trees. But that afternoon, I'm not sure why, we stayed indoors. His house was smaller than mine; a single room sheltered the entire family. On a table pushed into a corner of the room lay a magazine that I had never seen before, the *Best English Magazine*. 'This is the greatest Burmese magazine there is!' exclaimed Shafiul as he handed it to me. Apparently there was only one shop, run by a Buddhist in downtown Maungdaw, that stocked it nearby. Shafiul had to request one of his friends to bring him a copy.

As I leafed through the magazine, I saw quotes, poems, satirical pieces and translations of verses by famous authors. 'I've been writing for them the past few months,' Shafiul announced proudly. 'Look at this page, this is a poem I just published.' I could hardly believe it. We had spent so many afternoons together and this was the first time I realized that, like me, Shafiul was a writer. I was no longer alone; at last I had someone to share my secrets with.

Like a child in front of a toy store, I could hardly believe my eyes. Writing suddenly seemed like a possibility. Everything did. I too had to be published. Thrilled, I had lots of questions. How did he go about getting published? How did he get in touch with the magazine? How did he send the poems to them? Shafiul explained that he simply mailed the poems for a 50 kyats postage fee. The magazine was based in Yangon, so it typically took around fifteen days for the post to reach them.

Today, as I write these lines, I can safely say that afternoon changed the course of my life. Suddenly, a new world opened up to me, one where I could write, be published and allow myself to dream once again. I could live, feel alive, as though I had been resuscitated. They could very well erase my name, my identity, my culture, but writing would allow me to leave an indelible mark on the world. What had until then been only a nocturnal activity to calm my anxieties became the driving force of my days. I hadn't been able to go to university but I would become a writer, I promised myself.

In early May 2010, I posted two poems and five quotes to Yangon. As I handed over the envelope to the postman – a friend of my brother's – I felt the urge to hug him and explain how the simple pieces of paper within could change my life. The sap within me, long dried out, was regaining its vitality; my heart was beating again. On 12 June, I went back to Shafiul's house. I remember that day very clearly – unable to wait any long, I didn't even take the time to greet him. But he took great delight in making me wait, just to get on my nerves. After a few minutes, he finally showed me a page from the new issue of the magazine.

'Success'
Knowledge is candle
Lightening your life,
Brightening your brain
And...
Shining your future.

My eyes flicked to the signature next to the verse: M. Earthwar R. Ali. This was the name that I had chosen, my *nom de plume* at the time. 'M' for Mohammed, 'Earthwar' for my alias Akhter, 'R' for my real first name Rahmat and Ali, my family name. With my poem published, my identity had finally been recognized. I cried in joy, thinking about all those sleepless nights when I had toiled in the light of the lamp. Shafiul congratulated me. I couldn't stop flipping through the pages, wanting to read each word. The quote I sent in hadn't appeared but that didn't matter to me. I had been published. They could take our land, kill my grandfather, punish our children, prevent me from moving freely – but they could never erase my words. I kept repeating this to force myself to believe it. I finally existed and had found my path.

In time I discovered another magazine, *Light of English*, which encouraged young writers and opened me up to new perspectives. Within two years, I had published sixteen poems and over 200 quotes across both the magazines. The more I wrote, the more I wanted to read, learn and educate myself – I had developed a thirst for knowledge. I discovered poets that I looked up to, their stories resonating with my life. A whole new world was opening up to me. I learnt new words and feelings which freed my mind even while my body remained trapped in our oppressive state. I remember this quote from one of my favourite authors, Rabindranath Tagore, 'If you shed tears when you miss the sun, you also miss the stars.' Elsewhere, there were those who felt the same things as me – I was no longer alone. But I had to keep improving myself, perfecting my English, learning new subjects and along the way, find a path to university.

One summer morning in 2011, as I left the mosque in Boli where I now prayed everyday, I joined the elders in the shade of the trees, as was my habit. They were sitting and chatting about everything and nothing. My father stood next to his brother, Zakair. When my uncle noticed me, he asked, 'Tell me, how are your studies going? Were you able to decide what you want to study?'

I lowered my eyes, afraid that I might disappoint him. But when I looked up again, he was wearing a big smile. He looked like my father, which calmed me; gentle eyes, a balding head covered by a simple skullcap. He looked like a wise old man. He was slightly younger than my father, though they were often confused. He asked if I knew about distance education, an academic programme which would allow me to study university courses from home.

After some research, I learned that I would have to spend a month in Sittwe and take exams which would confirm my participation in the programme. I had been saving money for two years by giving English classes to children in my village – it was enough to fund a month's stay in the capital of Arakan. One week later, I was preparing to leave for Sittwe with Aziz, a friend of mine who wanted to attend the same course. He was a cousin of the Rohingya politician Aung Myo, and I told myself that we would have no trouble crossing the checkpoints thanks to his contacts. Aziz had meticulously planned the trip.

However, like every other time, we were insulted, humiliated and extorted. Fear can never be tamed no matter how much you train yourself. Words still resonate, looks haunt and gestures crush you over and over again. In front of the guards I was like a defenceless child; a chicken begging a hungry fox for mercy.

After the roadside inspections, we had to board an old wooden motorboat. We were seated in the hold with a few Buddhist people, including a young girl. She was magnificent, her fair skin decorated with thanaka paste that she wore like makeup. Her nails were painted, and she wore a floral dress that complimented her slender body. She was leafing through a copy of *Light of English*, the magazine I wrote for. I threw furtive glances her way which grew increasingly insistent. I wanted to tell her who I was, that she might have read my words. But she ignored me. I could feel her contempt or worse, indifference. To her I was nothing but an insignificant Rohingya, a nonentity.

Suddenly, I recognized my poem in the centre of the page that she was looking at.

What can I do ?

I can teach...

Hundred pupils

But I cannot teach...

A single heart !

I can control...

Hundred people

But I cannot control...

A single mind !

I can explain...

Hundred poems

But I cannot explain...

A single love !

I stayed silent. The government had successfully managed to create such a powerful divide between our two communities that this young girl, sitting only one seat away from me in an old tub, preferred to ignore me. What would she have said if she knew that she was reading the words of a Rohingya? Aziz noticed that I was upset and was pleased when I told him for the first time about my writing. He said, 'It's great for our community.'

The day was ending as we arrived in Sittwe; the night sky had begun to envelop the city. We took a rickshaw to Mow Lai, the Muslim neighbourhood. The air in the capital was cooler than in Maungdaw. The sea was very close to us and we could hear the waves. Everything looked bigger, the roads were wider, busier; the buildings looked taller and more colourful. We stopped in front of a hostel, requested a room and went straight upstairs. We were so tired we could hardly stand. I could see right as we entered the room that we needed to rearrange it. There were two beds in the room's centre. Muslims are forbidden to sleep with our feet pointing towards the west where the qiblah is situated, because it is sacred and should be venerated. Once the beds were aligned correctly, we were finally able to rest.

I looked at Aziz, who seemed very calm whereas I couldn't shake off that fear deep inside me. I was happy but kept thinking about the inspections. When I tried to talk about them he said, 'Only God will decide. Our destiny is in Allah's hands my friend, we can change nothing. In your case, God willing, you will be a great writer.'

His words had an air of resignation. It wasn't the first time that I'd heard statements of this kind. Many Rohingyas had learnt to accept this fate, our doomed fortunes; this submission that constantly oppressed us and prevented us from living like other human beings. I was disappointed with Aziz's reply. In my view, it was unacceptable. But what else could we do? I was too tired to respond to his comment that evening.

We stayed for a whole month in Sittwe. During the day we went for classes and took the required tests. In the evenings, we studied in our room. I remember very little of that period; time went by so fast. I often stayed in the room, immersed in books, and didn't enjoy the city. I only remember my last days there, like premonitory flashes. I had just finished the final English exam. I was the last student to leave the room, and I was satisfied, knowing I would pass. A group of about ten young Buddhist students from my class were waiting to ask me how the exam had gone. Or rather, to mock me and point fingers at me. I had a feeling that they were going to start beating me. Once again, I felt humiliated. Fortunately, the professor arrived and accompanied me to a rikshaw. A few other girls were with us. I was shaking, my heart pounding in my chest, I kept thinking about the stupid students who had treated me like dirt. This final image of the university has stayed with me – a place that allowed me to dream and where today we remain divided.

Before leaving the city, we went to buy some gifts for our families. The main market, run by Buddhists, was much bigger than the meagre stalls in our village. There were clothes, perfumes, posters and shoes galore. A T-shirt caught my eye but it wasn't the right colour.

When I approached the uninterested vendor, he stared back at me with fierce eyes and with a hint of hostility. I understood immediately. He did not want to show us his goods because we were Muslims. We thought it best to leave the market without buying anything, since no one wanted to sell their merchandise to us. This is my last memory of Sittwe, and the last time that I set foot there. Not long after, the neighbourhood of Mow Lai where we had stayed for a month would be destroyed. Hundreds of thousands of displaced Rohingyas would be forced out, to languish in squalid concentration camps along the Bay of Bengal.

8

Thought of ending life is common.
I might forget his feature,
Shall never I forget
How he made me feel in my boyhood.

– MAYYU ALI, 'The Nasaka and a Rohingya'

ONCE BACK HOME, I had a new goal; to do everything possible to get my degree. My prayers, the correspondence courses, then writing in the evenings – there was a rhythm to my days. My parents were suffering. We had been short of money ever since we'd lost our lands and I often saw my mother crying in the kitchen while cooking. Our family would no longer be able to sustain for very long; food supplies were dwindling and the new restrictions that prohibited our community from moving about freely or cultivating our own land did not bode well for us.

A few of my neighbours worked for non-governmental organizations, or NGOs. Since the 1990s, owing to renewed episodes of violence against us and policies of forced labour that drove numerous Rohingyas to Bangladesh, several NGOs had come to our rescue. Not only did they ensure that we had what we needed to survive – including free medical treatment, without which the list of deaths would have been much longer – but they also offered us new avenues for employment. Those of us who had the opportunity to go to school could apply to work with these NGOs. The added bonus was that the salaries they offered were much higher than public sector jobs, which were mostly off-limits to us regardless. Besides, in our community working with Westerners – the *feri* as we call them – is a matter of immense pride, a sort of accomplishment in itself.

I remember the first feri I saw. I was eight years old, still in primary school. Khin Nu, our teacher, had informed us the day before that humanitarian workers from Doctors Without Borders (DWB) would be visiting us to diagnose cases of malaria. It was a very dangerous disease – at that time, many people living in the most remote areas, in the mountains and close to rivers, were dying from it. Our teacher randomly selected around ten students, and I was among them. I was happy that I would finally see a foreigner, even though the country had been closed to the outside world for decades.

I was rushed into a room where a tall white lady,

sitting on a stool, was holding consultations. I looked very carefully at her. She was taller and sturdier than my mother. As I got closer, I observed that her features were thicker than those of the other women I knew. I noticed a thin layer of fine, blonde hair on her rosy cheeks. Her blue eyes bulged out of their sockets – I had never seen eyes of that colour before. Disheveled, straw-yellow hair fell around her shoulders. She seemed very strange to me indeed. She held out her hands and I was suddenly afraid; her skin was so white that I could see the green lines of her veins. I couldn't even tell the transparent gloves that she was wearing from her skin.

She introduced herself but I do not remember her name. My eyes were fixed on the packet of candy on the table behind her. She allowed me to eat a few, but not all at once. I peeled off the wrapper that covered the candy and let the sweet melt on my tongue for as long as possible; I wanted the sugar to spread through my entire palate. I had never eaten anything so sweet and creamy. While I was relishing it, the doctor took out her syringe and pricked my middle finger. I was so startled by this gesture that I munched the candy all at once.

'The test is negative. That's great news. Good luck my dear, take care of yourself and your family,' one of her colleagues translated for me. She waved her hands to say goodbye. I looked at her one last time before heading back to my class to share the candies with my classmates. I kept one that I gave to my mother as I told her the whole story that evening. DWB won the Nobel Peace Prize that year, in 1999, just as Aung San Suu Kyi had eight years earlier for her non-violent opposition to the military junta.

I too wanted to be useful, to help my people and those who were most vulnerable. In December 2011, Action Against Hunger (AAH) was looking for four people to work under their nutrition programme at the Maungdaw office. My neighbour and friend Reyas, who was already working for AAH, helped me write my CV and cover letter but I wasn't selected. More than 300 candidates had applied for just four positions. But I didn't give up. I continued to apply everywhere: AAH, DWB, the United Nations High Commissioner for Refugees (UNHCR), the World Food Programme (WFP), Malteser International and many others. I was never shortlisted. What more did I have to do? Reyas advised me to never give up; my chance would come. In May 2012, AAH was once again looking for five recruits. I submitted my application – my thirty-seventh in the span of a few months – and was hired as an agent for their therapeutic feeding programme.

The very next day, we were summoned for a five-day training programme. With me were Omar Faruk and Anuwar, who came from the district of Maungdaw. A car was waiting for us in front of a shop to take us to the office in Buthidaung, an hour and half away. On our journey, after the first checkpoint, we didn't have to get out of the vehicle. For the first time in my life, I could move freely without being insulted. I looked out the window and the curve of my lips immediately revealed my happiness. Anuwar shook me and asked why I was smiling to myself like an idiot. 'Now is the time to smile,' Omar interrupted him. 'They aren't stopping us anymore. If we're not happy today, we will never be!'

The training programme covered many topics: the benefits of breastfeeding, different types of nutrients, personal hygiene, vaccination and so on. Everything seemed interesting to me. On the second day, 3 June, things took a turn. As I returned to my room in the inn where I was staying, I saw my host listening to the radio. He was always glued to his radio. It was our only connection to the outside world – we had neither the Internet nor television and still fewer people had phones. He had a serious expression and didn't pay any attention to me, which was quite unlike him. The radio announced that eight Muslim pilgrims had been massacred by Rakhines in Taungu that day. They were travelling from Yangon by bus and had been killed on the way by Buddhist extremists.

Muslims from Yangon often came on pilgrimage to our

state. At the time, I was unaware that this tragic episode was in fact the starting point of the intercommunal violence which would wreak bloody havoc on our state in 2012, like the dark clouds that appear just before a storm. The government, however, used a different pretext to justify the attacks. Several sources spread the rumour that a Buddhist woman had been raped by three Muslim men on 28 May. According to official media, the Rohingya killings were only a consequence of this rape, nothing more. If you attack us, we retaliate – that is what they seemed to be saying.

At the end of our training, Omar Faruk and I planned to return home the same evening. He was originally from Myo Thu Gyi village, close to Maungdaw. After lunch, we both went to the mosque for Friday prayers. When we returned to the office, we saw several people standing by the door, including Khine Linn Tun, one of our Buddhist colleagues in charge of logistics. He held his cell phone in the middle, and everyone lowered their heads to hear the audio playing. 'There is a fire in the city centre of Maungdaw!' someone shouted, their voice hoarse. The noise was garbled but we could grasp a few appalling words: gunfire, murder, flames … 'Kalar, kalar!' screamed a man with a Buddhist accent.

We had all gathered now in the office compound. Something was happening in downtown Maungdaw. We heard there had been fire, shooting and fights but we didn't know exactly what could have triggered this new attack. The management decided to cancel the afternoon training session. News kept trickling in. At one point we heard that Omar's village was perishing in flames. Distraught, he held his head in his hands to avoid meeting our eyes, as if the burden he had to bear was already too heavy. We didn't know what to do except pray.

That same evening, a convoy was headed to Maungdaw. Omar made his decision – he was going to leave with them. 'I don't have time to think. I am worried about my mother, she's all alone,' he said. 'I cannot leave her, she's far too old to fend for herself. If something were to happen to her, I'd never forgive myself.' He was already in the car before I could respond. I wasn't sure what to do. Stay there fearing I'd never see my parents again, or go back unsure if I'd be able to reach my house at all?

I thought of my parents. Were they still breathing? I had no way of knowing, and it was driving me crazy. My mother's face haunted me. I could picture her in distress since she hadn't heard from me – she could not sleep a wink when I had to be away even for one night. I decided to go back to the inn to rest. There was nothing more I could do for the moment. The innkeeper tried her best to comfort me. She could understand my situation; she too hadn't heard from her daughter, Sheik Sena, who worked at the AAH office in Maungdaw.

Before nightfall, the Nasaka were deployed everywhere; their troops patrolling the villages, down to the nooks and crannies of every house. From my room window, I saw armed guards lining the street and tracked the piercing light of their Jeep headlights as they moved. They stopped from time to time and jumped out of the vehicles, like birds of prey swooping down for a kill. Were they going to kill us? Set fire to the inn? And my parents, were they still alive? I convulsed with fear. I could feel the muscles in my thighs and arms tighten and spasm, my stomach tied up in knots. I could no longer control anything, neither my body nor my mind, which was imagining the worst. I saw my mother suffering, completely covered in blood. That night, I believe I descended into a kind of madness.

At dawn, I was served a plate of fried noodles and some tea, like my mother would have done after a sleepless night. My host came over, radio in hand, and sat next to me on the bed. 'I know you haven't slept. But you need to pull yourself together. The situation could have been much worse today. The police fired on some Rohingyas in downtown Maungdaw. A few houses were also set on fire.' I felt like there was nothing left that I could hold onto. I let my entire body fall backwards. I wanted to disappear, only to wake up and realize that it had all been a bad dream.

On Monday I went back to the AAH office. Perhaps work would help me think about something else, since there was nothing else that I could do. The outpatient centres were closed, only the stabilization centre – where we treated children suffering from severe malnutrition – remained open. A colleague suggested that I join him there. To do so, I had to avoid the soldiers by taking back roads and alleys.

At the new centre, I met Nasima and Sabair. Nasima was one of the only Rohingya women working for a humanitarian organization. Very few women hold jobs in our culture, most stay home to raise their children. I met about ten stunted children with swollen bellies, like all those suffering from famine. Two babies – twins – were screaming in pain. Their mother no longer had enough milk to feed them. I helped as best I could by making energy drinks for them.

By lunchtime, I still couldn't get the images from the day before out of my head. Nasima sensed my mood. She had been widowed several years ago, after her husband tried to escape the violence by fleeing to Malaysia. His boat had capsized. His was one among the thousands of tragic stories of people seeking exile who are duped by unscrupulous smugglers.

Sabair was a nice man – the two of them made a good team. He was a native of Taung Bazar, a rural area situated to the north of Buthidaung. He suggested that I go with him to his village. From there, he would help me cross the mountains to reach my parents. It was a risky idea – the mountains were treacherous, only navigable by a sinuous road. Armed attacks by gangs were rampant, even more likely against this backdrop of violence.

On 10 June, the local authorities declared a curfew from 10 p.m. to 6 a.m. in the townships of Maungdaw and Buthidaung for a period of two months. The central government sent in soldiers to prepare for any backlash. They were easily identifiable by the scarves that they wore around their necks during emergencies – red to match the colour of the Burmese flag. That evening, around 9 p.m., I heard gunshots. This time around, they weren't garbled sounds over a telephone but live ammunition being fired just a few hundred meters away from my bed. I rushed out of my room to join my host. His head was resting on one of his hands and with the other, he held the radio to his ear. The host announced that two Rohingya boys had been shot dead by the army in Buthidaung as they were going to buy betel nut from a Rohingya-run shop. The incident took place around 8:40 p.m., though the curfew was at 10 p.m. Why then did the army shoot the boys? I felt cold, my hands were shaking. My host took a blanket and gave it to me so I could go back to my room and rest.

On 12 June, Buddhist extremists attacked some Rohingya villagers in Sittwe. There was no end to the violence and the days of terror seemed endless. It had already been fourteen days since the riots had begun. I didn't know the exact number of victims – movement was curtailed and journalists had no access to the area.

Then one morning we heard that the market in the city centre had been reopened. A few people stepped out into the streets. I had to find a way to use a telephone to reach my parents. I went to meet Maung Myint Lwin, AAH's logistics assistant, because he had the organization's phone with him. I explained everything, asking if I could make a phone call – just one to reassure my poor mother. He agreed. I dialled my uncle Zakair's number, since he had a phone with an antenna. My heart was beating really fast. Finally, someone answered.

It was my aunt Rashoo, Zakair's wife. She stayed silent for a moment before breaking into sobs. I wanted to console her but above all, to ask her to put me through to my parents. My mother called me back a few minutes later. I kept telling her not to worry anymore; I was safe and would come back when the situation calmed down.

On 22 June, I learned that a bus was arriving in Buthidaung to bring back teachers who had been stuck in Maungdaw during the curfew. I could go back; I could finally go home! Within a few hours, I had packed my things and bid farewell to the couple who had hosted me. On the bus, I could hardly believe it – I was well on my way back home. But every scene along the way was heartbreaking. I saw nothing but police officers at every street corner, every intersection, every turn. Apart from them the road was empty. Nobody wanted to move about – there weren't any children playing, nor any shopkeeper selling vegetables on display. It was as if life had been suspended.

When I got off the bus, I walked through the village market. There was no one there, something I had never seen before. On the doorstep of our house, my young nephews and nieces were waiting for me, shouting '*Futubaa ashe*!'[1] I couldn't stop myself from crying when I saw my mother looking for me. She kissed my forehead and hugged me tight, very tight. Her tears streamed down my shoulder. My father stood behind her and put his hand on the nape of my neck. 'Take off your shirt,' my mother said. 'I'll wash you with my own hands.'

She brought a metal pot filled with water. I wondered what she could be doing; she hadn't bathed me since I became an adult. 'This is golden water, gold dipped

---

[1] Younger father

water,' she told me. 'The water thus becomes precious just like the metal. When a person survives danger, we perform this ritual. This is our tradition, my son. It means that the life of the survivor is more precious than gold.' My mother massaged my body, her tears mingling with the golden water.

At home, peaceful in my cocoon, I hadn't forgotten what I had witnessed. Hundreds of men had been arbitrarily arrested and accused of setting fire to their homes or those of their neighbours. Dozens of Rohingyas had been shot dead by security forces. In retaliation, some Rohingyas had killed Buddhists, for which the Buddhists had taken revenge on Muslims. It had become a vicious cycle, an infernal cycle. The government's plan was working perfectly, to incite violence and hatred between two communities that had long been close and united. As of 22 August 2012, according to the Human Rights Watch (HRW), there were eighty-eight victims: fifty-seven Muslims and thirty-one Buddhists. About 90,000 people had been displaced and 2,528 houses burnt down, of which 1,336 belonged to Rohingyas and 1,192 to Rakhines.

9

A people

Since decades

For being Muslims minority

Still under blade and bullet

Still in hostile oppression

Still in rape and incarceration

Still in fire and fear

Ah ! What violence !

– MAYYU ALI, 'People Stateless Are Without World'

THIS CONFLICT ROBBED US of our happiness, our friendships, our aspirations and the people we loved. I never heard from Aung Naing, my childhood friend, again. I often thought of him. What was he up to? What did he think of all that was happening? Did he hate me like everyone else? Was he afraid of me now, he who knew my parents and my entire family, who had eaten at our house dozens of times? We were both wrecked by a wave of rebellion that had left us stranded on opposite shores.

Rohingya students were no longer permitted to attend Sittwe University. I witnessed processions of dead bodies, I heard rioters screaming. Would I be next on the list? I prayed, day and night, night and day, entrusting my fate in the hands of Allah. I sought His reassurance constantly, asking Him to help us.

The situation worsened by the day. Omar Faruk, my colleague from the Buthidaung office, was arrested along with his brother. They had been accused of setting fire to a shop on 6 June. He was with me that day, attending the training programme. Both brothers remained in prison for years.

Madrasas, markets and mosques were no longer allowed to operate. NGOs were prevented from functioning. The curfew stifled our lives; when the sirens rang at the end of the day, everyone had to return home until the next morning. Soldiers patrolled the villages from dusk until dawn, entering homes to arrest men whose only crime was that they were Rohingyas.

Violence resumed in October. This time, it was a coordinated campaign that aimed at forcefully eliminating all Muslim groups in the state. According to HRW, the conflict resulted in the deaths of at least 200 Rohingyas, the displacement of more than 1,40,000 people into open-air prisons in Sittwe and the burning down of thousands of houses.

AAH was no longer allowed to operate, and we were fired without any pay. The circumstances had become even more dire for me and all those who lived in remote areas. Everyone was at risk of famine. In the nutrition centres in Maungdaw, more than 70 per cent of the children under five years of age who had been screened were suffering from moderate malnutrition. Pregnant Rohingya women were losing weight week after week; young mothers were so weak that they were unable to breastfeed. We had a reserve of Plumpy'Nut® sachets – an energy paste that had been used across Africa during the great famines. By the end of the week, the children had already eaten through our supply. So dire was the food shortage that families often had to share a single sachet amongst them. The fathers were no longer allowed to fish or harvest their crops – they were helpless. No one was permitted to travel to the city centres. Numerous pregnant women died without any access to healthcare.

On 22 November 2012, a limited number of NGOs and UN agencies, including AAH, were given authorization to resume operations in restricted areas. I was called to the Maungdaw office, where I met the head of the human resources programme. They invited me to work there so I wouldn't have to worry about being stuck in Buthidaung anymore.

My colleagues Reyas, Siddique and I wanted to rent a house in the city centre. One evening, during our search, we met a Rohingya man who was an old friend of Siddique's. His name was Mohib Ullah and he was an advisor to the Association for the Regional Development of Buthidaung and Maungdaw, a social organization founded by Rohingya politicians. Ullah offered to help us find a place to live. I didn't know then that this encounter would change my life forever.

We followed him to the house. Rafique, the owner, had been arrested during the violence on 8 June and remained in the detention house in Buthidaung ever since. We were scared to linger for fear of attracting the police. Ullah immediately understood our predicament and changed the subject. He started talking to us about the impact of the violence on our community, like a father who wanted to counsel his children. 'This can't go on. They are killing us one by one. We must do something. Do any of you have data on the number of victims?'

'Since the incidents that took place on 8 June 2012, I have been collecting data on the victims and information on the violence perpetrated against the Rohingyas,' I replied. 'I only note what I can personally confirm. I wrote down the names of a few victims from Buthidaung. I recorded the number of people killed, arrested and imprisoned.'

'That's good, it's a good start. We must raise our voices now. Our people are experiencing several types of human rights violations, while the international community doesn't know what's happening. We need to raise an alarm, document these crimes and bring them before the arbiters of international justice. I work with a network of young people who are documenting the crimes. Would you be interested in joining us?'

Reyas seemed hesitant. As for me, it was clear that I finally had the opportunity to be useful to my community. 'Siddique, tell them what to do,' Ullah instructed. 'Be careful, they are everywhere, spying on the most educated amongst us.'

Siddique wasn't just a colleague, he was my friend. Four years older than me, he was relatively short and had fair skin like a feri. His mother was a Muslim woman from a different state and his father, a renowned trader, was native to Maungdaw. This was all he told me about them – he was discrete, but we trusted each other and spent a lot of time together. Siddique often said that he dreamed of becoming a great advocate who could 'defend our cause and advocate for our rights.' That, however, remained a distant utopia. Since 1970, Rohingya students no longer had the right to major in disciplines like medicine, law and engineering. This was meant to prevent us from pursuing more reputable professions.

My brother for instance had to study chemistry instead of medicine.

One Saturday in December 2012, Siddique and I met for lunch at a restaurant. I brought along one of my poems that I had wanted him to read for a long time. It was my first poem on the pain and suffering of our people.

'People Stateless Are Without World'
A people
Since centuries
Has been dwelling in Arakan,
But for being Muslim minority
Not allowed to survive on their ancestral land.
And under restriction and persecution
And still in exile.
Ah ! What apartheid !
No leader advocates about their national rights.
Is Myanmar without loyalist ?

A people
Since decades
For being Muslims minority
Still under the blade and bullet
Still in hostile oppression
Still in rape and incarceration

Still in fire and fear.
Ah ! What violence !
No whistle-blower proposes anything against it,
Is the world without independent investigation ?

A people
Since decades
Due to ghastliness of oppressive exile
Leave the land to escape for lives

Seeking refuge in neighbouring countries.
But for being Muslims minority
Few country bears providing refuge.
Ah ! What an adventure !
Are all states completed with own nations ?
Is not there a space to settle on the earth ?

A people
Since centuries
For being Muslims minority
Yet stateless
Having on the same earth
And under the same sky.
Why some of us are yet stateless ?
Thus, Rohingyas can be considered
Not only without state
But also without world !

I didn't know where to publish my poem. I couldn't send it to the magazines I wrote for anymore. They would realize it was written by a Rohingya, identify and arrest me. Siddique wasn't sure how to respond but asked to borrow my poem to show it to his friends who, like me, were writers.

A week later, when we were eating lunch at the same place, I was keen to know what his friends had thought of the poem. Siddique was trying to enjoy his bowl of curry but I refused to let him eat in peace, I was too curious. His friends had loved it, he said, some had even cried. They'd rarely read such a well-written text and were proud of me for composing it.

But my friend suddenly took on a serious air. He wanted to share something that was highly confidential and asked me to swear that I'd keep it to myself. I was perplexed. He brought his head closer to mine and put his hand in front of his mouth so that no one could read his lips. 'You must swear to Allah to never share this information with anyone,' he whispered in a Rohingya dialect.

'Of course, I promise, even under torture I will not breathe a word.'

'Do you remember your discussion with Mohib Ullah, the one who wanted to help us find a house?'

'Yes, yes of course.'

'Well, I'm part of that network. We've been working for many months to bring justice to our people. The basis of our claims is that we must remain non-violent and everything must go through the courts. What we do is ultimately quite simple. We collect information from the victims and send it abroad for publication.' He added, 'One last thing, we have no funding. We fund the entire operation from our pockets.' Siddique gave me a week's time to tell him whether I wanted to participate.

What they were doing was important and judicious. The international community did not know how much we were suffering on a daily basis. However, if I chose to join them, I would no longer be able to go home on weekends and would instead have to attend all their meetings. What was I going to tell my parents? My father would never want me to become a part of such activities – he was already afraid that I listened to the radio in public and accused me of meddling in politics. Despite my hesitations I could not let go of this opportunity. I believed in peace, I believed in the non-violent movement and above all, I wanted to help my community.

The next Sunday, I attended my first meeting with Siddique. We were seated in a room on the ground floor of a house, in a semi-circle. There were five other young men I had never seen before and whom I greeted with a shy handshake. I was impressed. They appeared well-dressed and modern, in jeans and shirts like most educated young people, while rural people preferred longyis.

Everyone recited the oath before Allah in our dialect, and in unison: '*Allahrégobá gori hoiddé*' (we swear before Allah). I followed easily, since Siddique had explained to me what I would have to say.

'Forget your name. From this point forward, you are R-16,' the man who appeared to be the director of operations told me. 'Each one of us has a code name. I must remind you that all this has to remain confidential.'

After brief introductions, we decided who would take charge of the next meeting and the week's activities. Then we discussed a variety of topics like the recent acts of violence, international justice and the importance of ensuring the safety of our members. The network was very well organized and even had its own code of conduct:

> Any member who comes fifteen minutes late to a meeting will have to pay a fine of 1,000 kyats. A member who is absent without a legitimate reason will be fined 2,000 kyats. Every member has to contribute 5,000 kyats per month to our fund. You will never share your experiences about the network,

even under the threat of death. This is the condition of our survival.

The network collected information every day, about arrests, imprisonments, rape cases and other violations of human rights committed against our people in Arakan. We relayed all verified information to Rohingyas living abroad who were actively working for our community, as well as to activists and human rights defenders who had taken an interest in the Rohingya cause.

Without access to the Internet, it was extremely difficult to make inquiries in the most remote areas of our region. We had to convince our acquaintances and neighbours to collaborate with us and keep us informed about every case. To do this, we equipped them with telephones that we paid for and Bangladeshi SIM cards. The border was so close that we could connect to the network there. It was painstaking work to cross-check every new activity and act of violence. It took a lot of time but I felt that we could, in this way, document the most serious crimes and bring the offenders to justice.

My poem 'People Stateless Are Without World' was published on the website www.rohingya-blogger.com. It was my first poem of activism, the first proof of my resistance. But I had to adopt a pseudonym in compliance with the rules of the network – the nom de plume by which my struggle would be known and hopefully recognized. The name I chose had to live up to my aspirations. I wanted it to bear the suffering of my people, to showcase our identity to the entire world. My name would have to tell our history to the people of the world.

I chose Mayyu Ali. 'Mayyu' comes from *moyur*, a Rohingya term for 'peacock'. Legend has it that there are many peacocks in the chain of mountains that separate Buthidaung from Maungdaw. It is called Moyur Far in Rohingya, or the Mountain of Peacocks. I've always found that very poetic. The river that flows along these mountains, across Maungdaw and into Naf and the Bay of Bengal is called the Mayu river. Besides, the peacock is a national symbol of Myanmar. The word 'Mayyu' is the emblem of the Rohingyas in Arakan. This is who I am. I can feel it – in my veins, in my blood. Every time someone calls me Mayyu, I feel alive.

We began compiling the instances of violence against our people. Since 2012, the violence had not stopped. The deadliest attack was in Du Chee Yar Tan, a village on the border of Maungdaw, that went on from 9–14 January 2014. The first day, the Buddhist inhabitants of the village attacked and killed eight Rohingya inhabitants. On 13 January, the Rohingyas captured and killed a police officer. In retaliation, hordes of Buddhists attacked residents with knives, sticks and firearms, killing everyone in their path. According to HRW, police authorities had verbally issued a general order authorizing the arrest of all Rohingya men and boys over the age of ten in the area. DWB reported having treated twenty-two Rohingya patients from the region who had suffered gunshot, knife and machete wounds. The UN confirmed that at least forty-eight Muslims had been killed in the attack, a massacre that the Myanmar government has consistently denied.

When the government learnt that DWB was providing aid to the victims, it immediately suspended their activities, accusing them of favouring the Rohingyas at the expense of other civilians. Pierre Peron, spokesperson for the United Nations Office for Coordination of Humanitarian Affairs (UNOCHA) publicly declared that DWB's departure from Myanmar had 'a serious humanitarian impact'. After eight months of struggle, DWB was able to resume its operations but its members were now seen as enemies. Many demonstrations were carried out against DWB and other NGOs. Cries of protest echoed:

'Go away, DWB!'

'NGOs get out of our country!'

'Get out UN!'

The logos of some international organizations were

symbolically defaced in our region, while the offices of DWB and Malteser in Sittwe were attacked and demolished. Our sole allies – the only ones who cared about the plight of the Rohingyas – had become targets themselves.

10

How we're thrilled faking a smile
When others are dying !
Is that human moral ?

– MAYYU ALI, 'Teardrops on My Book'

I HAVE ALWAYS TRIED to be understanding of others, even the worst criminals. To understand, though not excuse, allows us to avoid making the same mistakes and be more accepting of their impact on us. At one point, I tried to think like Aung Naing, my Buddhist neighbours, the government and its soldiers. What could have been going on in their heads? How can a man wake up in the morning, play with his child, wish him a good day and a few hours later, take a machete and kill another man's child? How does he continue to walk, live and breathe with blood on his hands? Without any guilt, without discerning good from evil. Does he stop being moved by the morning dew, the breeze on his skin or the feeling of holding his mother in his arms – these little things that make us alive? Humanity has disappeared, I thought, and wrote a poem about my troubles.

'Teardrops on My Book'
Days are going on.
Trust and value of men are melting down.
The impurity in the hearts of mankind
That fades away the beauty of human nature.
How we're thrilled faking a smile
When others are dying !
Is that human moral ?
Hiding a truth in heart is a foetus of great lie.
Thus, I too believe about those days in life.
But never I imagined that
It'd be so swift in these ways.
And day by day,
A new wave of atrocity comes to strike away.
Man sucks men's blood.
Governors annihilate civilians' dwells.
Indeed, mankind turns to wilder.
And quite against the light of morality
And I feel that it's my own.
That I want to author as I'd do.
But too heinous to take in my soul
And I lose all control.

My hand begrudges to take hold.
My fingers tame to ink bold.
And teardrops on my book
Lives are passing on.
Love and kindness of men are vanishing on.
The ignorance in the thoughts of human beings
That wanes out the grace of human etiquette.
How we're apathetic seeing in silence
When others are being eliminated !
Is that human virtue ?
Breeding a hatred in heart is an offspring of great pogrom.
So, I too believe in man-made disasters.
But never I thought that
It's be so ruthless in such ways.

And day by day,
A fresh catastrophe comes to exterminate.
Man takes men souls.
Race hectors each other.
Indeed, mankind turns to cruller.
And quite against the charm of humanity
And I feel that it's my own.
That I want to count on as I'd do.
But, too perilous to take in my heart
And I stifle all breath.
My hands envy to take hold of the pen

But it slips down on the spot.
And teardrops on my book.

The government, soldiers and executioners infiltrated and polluted the minds of the people with the most effective instrument: religion. In a country that is 90 per cent Buddhist, monks became thought leaders and anti-Muslim sermons in monasteries became common. They became more radical and vindictive, singling us out as their arch-enemy. Buddhism in Myanmar started to go hand in hand with extremism. It even had a name that inspired terror: Ashin Wirathu. Imprisoned in 2003 for inciting racial hatred, this *bhikkhu*[2] was released in 2012 and joined the Ma Soe Yein monastery in Mandalay, the heart of the country. He then took charge of the 969 movement, which called to boycott shops run by Muslims, buy Burmese goods and strengthen the 'Burmese race'. In Buddhism, the number 969 represents the three jewels of the Buddha: his image, teachings (Dharma) and finally the Buddhist spiritual community (Sangha). Today it symbolizes nationalism and radicalism instead.

The 969 movement spread across the country. Towards the end of March 2013, the city of Meiktila became the epicentre of violent massacres between Buddhists and

---

[2] Buddhist monk

Muslims. More than forty people were killed and fires ravaged mosques and Muslim homes. The number '969' was spray-painted on the debris. Other attacks took place in several cities in a central region of the country, Bago. It was as though the whole of Myanmar had been infected by the same virus: hatred against Muslims. Within our network, we observed that violence often occurred after visits from Wirathu or his disciples. Meanwhile, Wirathu – who calls himself the 'Burmese Bin Laden' – described the carnage in Meiktila as 'a demonstration of force'.

I saw 969 stickers for the first time in 2013. Suddenly, they were everywhere: at the entrances to Rakhine villages, on Buddhist shop windows and even cake boxes. Wirathu often came to Sittwe and visited Maungdaw and Buthidaung on occasion. Bhikkhus travelled from village to village on board cars and motorcycles, offering food, DVDs and propaganda brochures. According to them, we were the cause of all their problems: poverty, violence, lack of education and so on. They promised a better life once we were eliminated. I learnt that the 969 movement had also spearheaded several protests against NGOs and Rohingyas. Local leaders gave 5,000 kyats each to Buddhists and asked for their support when conducting protest marches on the streets of Maungdaw, for instance.

In 2013 the movement was banned by the authorities but shortly afterwards, Wirathu created a new organization. Ma Ba Tha, meaning 'Association for the Protection of Race and Religion'. As Internet access became more common in the country in 2014, Wirathu relied on social media networks to further propagate his message. Ma Ba Tha is highly structured and lobbied for the Race and Religion Protection Laws adopted in 2015, which limit the number of children Muslim couples can have and prohibit Burmese women from marrying outside their religion.

Videos of Wirathu's sermons are very popular. One of the most famous, in which he lectures hundreds of Buddhists seated as if in a trance, sums up their ideology:

'Is it better to marry a vagrant or a Muslim?' he asks.

'A vagrant!' the crowd roars.

'And is it better to marry a dog or a Muslim? A dog. Unlike a Muslim, the dog will never ask you to change your religion …'

The propaganda spread by Wirathu and his followers portrays Muslim men as sexual predators who rape Buddhist women or force them into marriage and conversion. The strategy they used to incite unrest was often the same. In a village, Muslim men would be accused of raping a woman and once the information was shared on social media, the region was set ablaze. Things would be allowed to go out of control, while numerous distorted and fake videos were circulated online.

The preachers had the freedom to post whatever they wanted, while we Rohingyas could be arrested simply for possessing a cellphone. In December 2014, for example, two members of our network were arrested by the police in downtown Maungdaw merely for using Facebook. They were charged with defamation. One was released in 2018, while the other remains in prison. All these movements and massacres couldn't have taken place without the consent of the army and the government, after all. The authorities opened the door to violence and hatred did the rest.

As we faced this wall built against us, I was inspired to pen down a few words.

'Myanmar mourns its men'

Which tribe ever you belong,
You, all are in the same heart
Paying the same blood
And the same sweat
Thus, no quite uniqueness
Between each of you have.
You are the one who makes me worthy.
You are the one who makes me insolent.

Oh my people !

Do not assail each other.
Do not make me embarrassed !
Do not make me degraded !
Which complexion ever your skin has,
You, all are in the same garden,
Having the same soil
And the same water
Thus, no quite feebleness
Between each of you have
You are the one who makes me glorious.
You are the one who makes me impudent.

Oh my people !
Do not bully each other.
Do not make me embarrassed !
Do not make me degraded !

Which royalty ever you possess,
You, all are under the same sky
Having the same air
And the same shadow
Thus, no quite divergence
Between each of you have
You are the one who makes me arrogant.
You are the one who makes me impertinent.

I would have liked the Buddhists to read my words, to understand that ultimately, we are only people like them. Instead, we let horrible things happen, a little worse every day. In allowing these horrors to repeat, in getting used to them, they became commonplace, ordinary and unremarkable. Their strategy was to divide and rule. Didn't Hitler do the same thing in Europe?

11

Yesterday…
When she was in detention,
She had to say to the world…
"Please, use your liberty for ours."
And the world used it for her.
Now, she has her liberty !

– MAYYU ALI, 'Her Yesterday and My Today'

THE 2015 GENERAL ELECTIONS were approaching. Our only hope had two names, Aung San Suu Kyi and her party, the National League for Democracy (NLD). The atmosphere was buzzing with excitement as our idol, who stood for courage, selflessness, passion, strength and freedom, was finally back at the forefront of national politics.

For many months, she had led an election campaign with one watchword: national reconciliation. I remember her speech in the Parliament in July, in opposition to the regime in power. Her hands resting on the lectern, with a haughty bearing to better defy her competitors and flowers in her hair, she spoke the following words: 'To become a truly democratic union, I call upon all the members of the Parliament to discuss the implementation of the necessary laws to protect the right to equality of ethnic groups.'

Guerrillas were wreaking havoc across the country. Every border area was simmering with conflict as separatist groups fought the army. Aung San Suu Kyi promised to bring peace once she was elected to power. I was certain that she would ultimately recognize us Rohingyas as full-fledged citizens and restore our dignity.

During Aung San Suu Kyi's campaign she visited several villages. The locals, many of whom were seeing her for the first time, screamed, 'Mother Suu, mother Suu!' She was like a rockstar surrounded by fans. Not only a politician – she was our icon, our mother. Though she hadn't scheduled a visit to Arakan before the elections, she had all our support. My mother and I never missed any of her speeches. I asked my mother one evening who she was going to vote for. Her answer was clear.

'You know, during the 1990 elections, your grandfather welcomed politicians to our home. He invited them to eat with us and sacrificed cows and goats. He was convinced that one day Aung San Suu Kyi would bring democracy to Myanmar, which is why he always supported her and it is my turn to support her now,' she explained. 'During the 1990 electoral campaign, your grandfather toured several villages to convince people to vote for the NLD. It was quite a sight to see him brimming with enthusiasm and determination. He believed with all his heart that Suu Kyi would save us. Her party indeed won the elections that year, even while she was under house arrest. But sure enough, the army, who wanted to maintain the status quo, annulled the elections. Your grandfather was furious.'

I remember my grandfather telling me about Aung San Suu Kyi's father, General Aung San, a hero of our independence struggle. He negotiated our independence with the British but was assassinated six months before he could witness it. The general accepted and recognized the Rohingyas, and wanted to unite the different ethnicities of the country. 'At the time,' my grandfather said to me, 'we used to have a radio programme in the Rohingya language.' He also told me that he threw a wonderful party when Suu Kyi received the Nobel Peace Prize in 1991. He took out an old portrait of hers for the occasion which was normally hidden in a cupboard. Under the junta, keeping a photo of Aung San Suu Kyi was punishable by imprisonment.

Each person in my family fought for the Lady from

Rangoon in their own way. While my grandfather did door-to-door visits, my older brother and one of my uncles went on protest marches to defend Aung San Suu Kyi's rights. My uncle was actually arrested twice during the general strikes in August 1988 for denouncing the junta and supporting Suu Kyi. Even peaceful demonstrations were violently repressed by the military. My uncle was detained and tortured for three days and eventually had to leave Myanmar.

Generation after generation, we have supported Aung San Suu Kyi. I remember a passage from the book she wrote during house arrest, *Freedom from Fear*. It greatly inspired me, especially since I was consumed by this feeling myself.

> It is not power that corrupts but fear. Fear of losing power corrupts those who wield it and fear of the scourge of power corrupts those who are subject to it ... A most insidious form of fear is that which masquerades as common sense or even wisdom, condemning as foolish, reckless, insignificant or futile the small, daily acts of courage which help to preserve man's self-respect and inherent human dignity. It is not easy for a people conditioned by the iron rule of the principle that might is right to free themselves from the enervating miasma of fear. Yet even under

> the most crushing state machinery courage rises up again and again, for fear is not the natural state of civilized man.

I was eager to vote and put an end to these years of oppression. Democracy would save us, and I would once again be able to dream, hope and grow. As a teacher, a writer, I would be able to represent my country, travel and get involved in politics. These things may seem trivial to those who have known the freedom I never had.

During the general elections in November 2010, the military junta permitted the Rohingyas – even those with temporary white cards – to vote. The village school compound where the voting took place was overcrowded; families brought their children along and there was so much noise. I still remember the moment when I slipped my ballot paper into the box and the clerk marked my finger with ink – proof of my presence on that historic day. I was so happy that I didn't want to wash my hands, to ensure that the moment would remain etched in my memory for as long as possible. The party formed by the dictatorship won a large majority of the seats in the new parliament. Four Rohingyas had been elected: Aung Zaw Win, Htay Win, Shwe Maung and Aung Myo Min. However, they could never assume responsibility since their election was declared null and void.

The upcoming elections – the first free elections in twenty-five years – marked a new era in the history of our country, bringing us one step closer to democracy. The polls were to be held on 8 November 2015. Then, on 2 November, we learned over the radio that Rohingyas who held temporary white cards were not authorized to vote. Aung San Suu Kyi had also expelled all Muslim representatives of her party. I couldn't believe it. Was she under some kind of pressure?

When Aung San Suu Kyi was released on 13 November 2010, people throughout the country could be heard singing. 'The Lady has been released. Hope has returned. Democracy has been liberated.' Looking back, I can say that preventing us from voting in 2015 was the first sign of Suu Kyi's cowardice. For a long time, we had believed that she refrained from taking our name to avoid shocking public opinion, so she could run in the elections and defend us better once she was in power. On the night of 9 November 2015, while many people celebrated the victory of the Lady from Rangoon and spoke about a new dawn, I sat on a chair outside. I was searching the night sky for a star – a sign of my grandfather – to share my anguish with him.

12

Rohingya Aid Workers
Being the victims for themselves,
Surviving in a modern Ghetto.
They those who support others,
Braving tremendous dangers
At risk, in great orders.

– MAYYU ALI, 'Rohingya Aid Workers'

AFTER THE ELECTIONS, I continued my humanitarian work with AAH. There were 400 people working in the Maungdaw and Buthidaung offices: Muslims, Buddhists, people from other cities in Myanmar and even foreigners. I felt fully appreciated whenever I was with them. I had never before experienced such solidarity. There were no differences between us. The colour of our skin didn't matter; religion mattered even less, and we never spoke about it. Each person respected the other, and for the first time in my life I felt like an equal. The time that I spent with my colleagues at AAH was my last experience of freedom and peace.

Some AAH workers took care of nutrition and others of mental healthcare, in addition to the medical team and healthcare centres. Three days a week, I slept at the Inn Din centre near Maungdaw. I shared my room with Kyaw Aye, a Buddhist from Magway in northern Myanmar. He was a little younger than me. He was always smiling and had a tiny mole under his nose. He worked for the medical team and I for the nutrition wing. We spoke to each other in Burmese and in English to the others.

After work, at 5 p.m., we would often go to the Inn Din market for drinks. We walked along the beach, with the sea in front of us and the sand still warm beneath our feet. Rohingya fishermen bobbed along on their moon boats and villagers came to buy fresh fish from the sea. It was nothing short of heavenly ... except behind the sandy beach there were graveyards of innocent people, gunshots muffled by the sounds of the waves.

In February 2016, I was promoted to data analyst and specialized translator in the mental health care programme, tasked with processing the information that we received. I had my own office and a personal computer – I was very pleased. I made several trips back and forth and spent two to three days a week there. On the way, we had to cross three checkpoints. Valerie, the AAH in-charge from the US, accompanied me. She supervised my work most of the time. She was about thirty years old, much taller and better built than me. She always spoke very fast and at first, I had to listen attentively to understand what she was saying. I soon got used to it.

By then, the rules had changed again. Rohingya humanitarian workers were required to have travel authorization and a professional identity card from their office. I always carried this card with me. That day there were around a dozen armed men in front of me. Though the Nasaka had been dissolved in 2013, we were still inspected every time. They were now called the paramilitary Border Guard Police (BGP). Only their uniforms had changed, everything else remained the same: the way they looked at us, their weapons, their insults, their disdain.

The officer refused to sign my authorization slip. 'You do not have the National Verification Card (NVC)?'

'No, I didn't take one,' I replied.

'Why not?'

'I don't need it to travel. I have a receipt for my white card, a photocopy of my AAH ID and a signed "Form 4", which authorizes Rohingyas to travel from one district to another. I have all the documents that are required,' I insisted. I tried to look confident as I spoke but deep down, I was scared.

'You are a Bengali. All Bengalis should apply for the NVC to live in our country!' He yelled so hard that his saliva splashed on my face. I was disgusted. Seeing that the situation was worsening, Valerie – who had been waiting in the car – came to my rescue. 'The next time you will not be allowed to cross without the NVC,' the guard said, holding back his anger in Valerie's presence. Back in the car, I stayed silent.

The NVC is a core issue of our struggle. It was and remains a symbol of the erasure of our identity. By accepting the NVC – generally given to immigrants – we accept being viewed as foreigners living in Myanmar. The government was trying to destroy our people through this administrative process, one that deprived us of our fundamental right to own property, vote or even stand in elections. Rejecting it was an assertion of our right to the land on which we have lived for centuries; to reject this denial of citizenship. However, many people were forced to accept the NVC on pain of death. For instance, fishermen who were prohibited to take out their boats without their cards, or farmers who could not cultivate their fields anymore. This card had become the first weapon of our genocide, an instrument used to deny our existence.

Valerie interrupted my thoughts to examine me from head to toe. I pretended that all was well but I've always been a terrible actor. Those who knew me were aware that I was terrified of these inspections. The only thing that calmed me down was writing. I'd recently got a smartphone and it had revolutionized my daily life. I could write anywhere, anytime. I wrote the rest of the way – a poem of rage, a poem of pain.

'Rohingya Aid Workers'
Being the victims for themselves,
Surviving in a modern Ghetto.
They those who support others,
Braving tremendous dangers
At risk, in great orders.
Whoever the needy is,
Their hands never discriminate,
And never give up.
Even for the hurdle of capital-based promotions
They work hard for well-being of multicultural community,
For their least-developed Northern Rakhine State.
In the offices,
They work together with diverse colleagues,
But nothing fades away their team spirits.
Having the sense of One Humanity.

The driver stops the car reluctantly.
They have to get off the car

To be under the check-up of authority
In out posts of the security.

'Why is my body checked ?
Even it has a heart to save many lives !
Why my back-bag is checked ?
Even it has tools to cure many lives !'
And they get on again,
Having the approval of entry.
For soon, they turn to their philosophy.
Then the experts see them back
With a round of empathy
'Are you okay ?' by saying !

Then they come back to their conscience
And bear a hard smile for their off faces.
And ever continue their humanitarian journey
In a very strong sense of commitment
Just rebuilding others' lives and dignities.

In August 2016, inspections at the checkpoints became stricter. The guards were becoming increasingly harsh, insulting and oppressive. Restrictions were imposed and we were threatened more than ever. The smallest pretext was good enough to torture a Rohingya and throw them into prison. The rule of law was replaced by force; we were condemned to a lawless zone.

I was living in a hostel with several friends in the city centre. Every evening after dinner we would talk about our fears. Ibrahim was the most concerned. 'Enose bhai, tell me, if the NGOs close down like last year, what will become of us?'

'Relax, don't worry. I can do anything to survive. If I don't work here anymore, I will pull a rickshaw cart to feed my family.'

I admired Enose bhai. He always took things in stride, one day at a time. He was the only one who helped us distance from all that we were facing. Though he was forty years old, he looked much younger than those of us who were constantly worried. He spent his time eating, joking and running around. He loved fashion and wore a cap, which was quite uncommon where we come from.

Despite these pleasant moments, the atmosphere was heavy and oppressive. We tried to keep our spirits high and lead a normal life, but every morning I woke up wondering if I was going to get killed that day. On 8 October 2016, I had a day like any other. That evening, I was too tired to write so I watched a Bollywood movie on my phone before falling asleep. At midnight, I was woken by a noise – the thunder of exploding bullets. I didn't know where it was coming from or what was happening. It started again, in the middle of my sleep. My nights had become a living hell.

As dawn broke, I heard more gunshots; sharper, closer to us. It turned out that the fighting was happening in the village of Myo Thu Gyi, six kilometres away from my hostel. My telephone started ringing. Omar Faruk, my friend who lived there, was panting. 'The army has killed seven young men, one of whom was sixteen years old. They were my neighbours. I don't know what to do, Rahmat. Help me!' he pleaded.

'Calm down and tell me more.'

'There are dozens of soldiers in the street, Rahmat. I have never seen so many of them before. Some of them are in trucks and ...' The call disconnected. I wanted to understand things more clearly. Why had the army shot seven Rohingya youth in Myo Thu Gyi? Who was responsible?

At breakfast, the topic was on everyone's mind. Enose bhai suggested that this could be the work of the Arakan Army. We looked at him. He was tense – it was the first time I'd seen him like that. He had just called his family, who had been victims of fighting between the Arakan Army and the government forces a few months earlier. The Army was created in 2009 by the Buddhist general Twan Mrat Naing to defend the interests of the Rakhine people. Close to 2,000 separatists are fighting alongside him even today to combat the 'Burmese colonization that is plundering our state' and advocate for the independence of Arakan. We had very little contact with this militia, though both our groups had been targeted by the government.

An announcement on the loudspeaker interrupted our conversation around 9 a.m.: 'The neighbourhood has been attacked by Bengali extremists.' Nobody dared to speak. Through the window, we could now see columns of smoke rising into the sky. The army was setting fire to Rohingya houses. As before, everything was stalled: markets, mosques, schools and NGO activities. But like Omar, I had never seen so many soldiers in the colony.

On 14 October 2016, Aung San Suu Kyi's office released the details of the 9 October attack. They claimed an armed Muslim group called Harakah Al-Yaqin had attacked three border posts and killed at least nine guards. The statement added that the Rohingya assailants acted on the orders of their commander Ataullah.

It was the first time that I'd heard of this group. I wondered who they were and what they wanted to achieve. Did they even exist or were they an invention of the authorities? The government announced the implementation of a 'cleansing operation' in Arakan coordinated by the Burmese Army and the police in three districts that were inhabited primarily by Rohingyas: Maungdaw, Buthidaung and Rathedaung. We had all become terrorists in their eyes. We were made to remove the fences in front of our houses so that everyone could see what we were doing. Emergency martial law was imposed from 9 p.m. to 6 a.m.

Before sunrise, the military would surround a Rohingya village they had identified a day earlier and start firing. If they found a knife, a black T-shirt or a pair of black pants while searching the houses, they would accuse the family of being connected with the attackers. All the members of the family would be arrested and sent to prison. But that was not all. To traumatize them so that they carried the scars of this horror for life, the soldiers raped the women and young girls one by one.

Another major event took place on 14 October. Security forces surrounded the home of Karim Ullah, a humanitarian aid worker who had been working for WFP and UNHCR in Maungdaw for many years. He was a good friend of my father's and often came to visit him. They arrested Karim and four of his sons, one of whom worked for WFP, and held them in custody. On 16 October, Karim was tortured to death by the police during an interrogation. His four sons were kept in Buthidaung Prison for years, accused of taking part in the terrorist attack even though they were all working that day. Like Karim, hundreds of educated people were tortured to death in police custody. I later wrote a poem about Karim Ullah's death, based on the account of his son who was released after two years.

'Torture'

Genocide's blade doesn't discriminate by age.
Who is young and strong
Male and educated,
He is abducted, tortured and sent to the grave.
My father and I were made stripped first,
Our hands were tied, we were hung up.
"Say as I say" the officer threatened.
Our tongues didn't want to lie.

"We're terrorists" They wanted us to confess.
They plucked each hair of my father's beards.
They set fire to my phallus with a lighter.
The eyes of my father were shutting down.

The prison is built on my father's land.
The prison that he built during forced labour.
Where he was tortured to death inside,
And I was imprisoned for years.

Not long after, my mother called me and I knew something bad was about to happen. Security forces were not far away and in my cupboard I had dozens of notebooks scribbled with personal notes that documented their abuse. She informed me regretfully that my father had decided to burn them all. My world stopped for a moment. Years of writing, burnt. It was as if my stomach was being ripped apart with the pages crackling in the flames.

The same day, 14 October, security forces burned down Ywama in Nga Sar Kyeu, a village in northern Maungdaw. Many young men were arrested, women and girls raped. The next day, security forces returned and repeated the same atrocities. A young girl was gang-raped in front of her father and left for dead. She continued to bleed in the aftermath and when her father tried to take her to the hospital, he was not allowed to cross the city. The girl died on 26 October from severe bleeding. Before her death she testified about the violence she had experienced.

> First, the soldiers asked for money and gold. I gave everything I had, even my gold earrings, still they raped me one by one. The last one said to me: 'I will not use my penis for you.' Instead, he used his knife. They left me for dead. I was bleeding and unable to speak.

Oo Shan Kyar, a Rohingya village north of the Maungdaw

town centre, was where the Burmese security forces raped the maximum number of women and girls. Our network reported that more than 120 Rohingyas had been raped in the village in December 2016. Our contact there gave us the following information: 'Dozens of rape victims are in serious condition. Some are still bleeding, they require urgent medical attention.'

Amid mounting atrocities, AAH opened an outpatient nutrition centre and another to hospitalize patients. Valerie and I visited both every day. We had a dedicated mental health team to help those affected by trauma, which my friend Reyas was part of. Our team reported that several debilitated women, pregnant women and young mothers had been suffering from severe mental health conditions since the implementation of the 'cleansing operation' and the violence that followed.

One Monday, Valerie and I attended one of the counselling sessions organized by AAH. She wanted me to act as a translator. Nearly all the patients were pregnant women. Among them there was an elderly woman who looked very withdrawn and fragile. She kept wiping her tears, hiding behind her veil. I told Valerie discreetly that we should go to her – she needed help.

Reyas brought us to a separate room so that the old woman could be at peace, speak freely and feel safe. 'Auntie, I am here to help you and listen to you.' Reyas spoke softly, trying to reassure her. 'You can tell us anything you want; it will not leave this room.'

The old lady turned to look at me. I smiled at her and said, 'I am here just for you. I am like your son. You are like my mother.' On hearing this, she broke down sobbing. Reyas gave her a handkerchief. The woman then showed him a small card. 'This is my daughter's ration card. She died last week during childbirth.' She paused to catch her breath, wiping her tears with trembling hands. Valerie was looking at me, but we didn't stop the woman from crying. We wanted her to calm down after having expressed her pain.

'Auntie, please continue. We want to know everything,' Reyas encouraged her.

'It was midnight. My daughter was about to give birth. I woke up and lit an oil lamp inside the house. We live in the mountains. When the security forces saw the light inside my house, they started shooting.'

I took out a bottle of drinking water. She drank some water. Though her hands were shaking, her tears still flowing, the woman spoke on.

'We turned off the lamp. My daughter was crying in pain. She started to bleed. We tried to get her to safety and on the way, she gave birth in the middle of the forest. My son-in-law found a bamboo wire to cut the umbilical cord, but it wasn't sharp enough.'

She paused once again. I looked at Valerie. We were all devastated by what we were hearing, but we certainly could not cry in front of the person who had endured it.

'Suddenly, the security forces opened fire once again. My son-in-law wanted to return home to bring something sharper. But I didn't allow him to leave, I was scared that he would get killed. So I cut the cord as best I could, and my daughter died of severe bleeding.'

I couldn't believe my ears – it was nothing short of a horror movie. Valerie hugged the old lady, who couldn't stop crying.

I heard dozens of such stories. As part of the so-called cleansing, the security forces committed unimaginable human rights violations. In the village of Long Don, security forces gang-raped dozens of Rohingya girls during a raid. In early November, the Burmese Army used helicopters to shoot at Rohingya villagers in the Pwint Phyu Chaung region of northern Maungdaw. Dozens were shot dead and hundreds more injured.

On 15 December, security forces burned down Kiyal Bil, a village close to my parent's house. People began to flee. The fire eventually reached my village, accompanied by the gunshots of our persecutors. My brother called me, terrified. I told him not to leave the house. It would be worse elsewhere.

I didn't want my family to flee. Where could they

go? They would be forced into exile, like thousands of others, in Bangladesh. After 1978, when our community began to take refuge in there, a Rohingya saying was born: 'Leave and you will die of hunger in Bangladesh.' Those who were lucky enough to return spoke about the horrific conditions in the camps – there was no food, absolutely nothing.

My brother called back at the end of the day to tell me that my family was leaving. They had no choice. They were being evacuated to Gainda Hali, a village situated beyond the Purma river in northern Maungdaw. Two days later, my parents were able to return after the forces left. Luckily, our house had not been damaged by the flames.

As per HRW, dozens of Rohingyas had been killed in the 'cleansing operation'. More than 1,200 houses were burnt, 30,000 people internally displaced. It was difficult to assess the situation, since the region was now off-limits to NGOs and journalists. The numbers had to be much greater, especially after mass graves were discovered in Nga Sar Kyue and Long Don.

I was still living in the hostel. On 17 December, I woke up early in the morning and looked out my window. I saw a hungry dog crossing the road against the misty sky. I then opened my phone, only to find images of the ongoing violence flooding social media. On Facebook, I saw the dead body of a child floating in the water. The child was wearing a shirt but his legs were bare. Soldiers had opened fire on a family who were trying to flee across the Naf river and the child had been killed. My heart stopped. I felt nauseous, sweaty – my sheets were wet. I started crying and just couldn't stop my tears; of anger, of pain. My head was aching, my back hurt. In that moment I remembered Aylan Kurdi, the three-year-old Syrian boy who had drowned in the Mediterranean Sea on 2 September 2015 while his family was attempting to reach Europe. I wrote these words:

A bullet in the chest bigger than a heart
A body falls into the water
The shooters dance on the riverbank
And the world just watches on.

My brothers, my sisters, my people were being killed with impunity. Death lurked all around us and the world looked on silently. We kept hoping for a new dawn, but it never came. The gradual extermination of our community continues. And with each passing day, I feel that a part of me dies with those that I have buried.

13

We cross the territory of death and dread
We are born to escape for life
I escape as best I could

– MAYYU ALI, 'Born to suffer'

ON 15 JANUARY 2017, DISTRICT Immigration Services started the annual census of our village with the goal of learning how many Rohingya families had fled to Bangladesh. I was still living in the hostel in downtown Maungdaw, working for AAH. There weren't any buses plying and regardless, my parents didn't want me to risk coming home, since the 'cleansing operation' primarily targeted young, educated Rohingyas like me. But I had to justify my absence from the census. When a family member failed to show up, the officers canceled the procedure. They also had the habit of extorting money; one had to, for instance, pay between 5,000 to 10,000 kyats if the family had a newborn. Despite a letter from one of my superiors, my father had to pay 2,000 kyats. The agents also demanded that I go to their office the following month or face harsher penalties.

A few weeks later, I stood before them. The landscape I encountered on my journey there was apocalyptic. Shops had been looted, the earth scorched. The odour of charred grass scalded my throat, along with that of cycle carcasses burnt to a cinder and houses reduced to ash. The smoky sky showed no sign of clearing – no light emerged from its gaps. It seemed like the first sign of an endless night. How many corpses had perished there? Where had the survivors gone?

As I sat on a chair in front of the immigration officer, my legs close together, I read the stories of the dead in his eyes. He was responsible too, like all the others who had been destroying our lives for years.

'You live in the city centre?' he wanted to know.

'Yes, I work for AAH.'

I gave him a letter of recommendation. He read it and took out my family's census file before signing my attendance certificate. A photographer took my picture. In front of me, on a small wooden board, my family number and my father's name were engraved. This would be the final proof of my life in Myanmar – my final trace on my homeland – and I didn't even know it then.

Following the 'cleansing operation' of October 2016,

several human rights associations and NGOs have accused Myanmar's government and military of crimes against humanity, including ethnic cleansing and sexual violence. The United Nations High Commissioner for Human Rights Zeid Ra'ad Al-Hussein declared on 11 September 2017, 'I call on the [Myanmar] Government to end its current cruel military operation, with accountability for all violations that have occurred and to reverse the pattern of severe and widespread discrimination against the Rohingya population.'

With the world's eye on us, pressure was mounting in Arakan. The government didn't want any information about what was happening on our soil to leak. During inspections, our telephones were checked and our contacts verified. I had to protect my personal notebooks, in which I had recorded the invaluable testimonies of the victims. My father had discarded several, but I continued collecting them. Sometimes I hid them in my hostel, other times at a friend's house or in the office. I met all the criteria for being arrested: I was educated, worked with an NGO and was in touch with both the foreign media and Rohingya diaspora.

In July, the authorities suspended WFP aid for Rohingyas in the north of the state. Those who benefitted from the programme in remote areas were the most affected; there was no one left to help them. We were left to starve again.

Wirathu came to Maungdaw in August 2017, where he met the chief of the border police. He visited many monasteries in the city. In the same month, Rakhine leaders – including Aye Maung – went to Naypyidaw, the capital of Myanmar. They met Min Aung Hlaing, the commander-in-chief of the army, and other nationalist parliamentarians. Their demand that security be reinforced in the northern regions of our state was accepted. On 22 August, several military trucks arrived in Maungdaw from Sittwe. Around 2,000 men were deployed in the districts of Maungdaw, Buthidaung and Rathedaung.

On 24 August, I was at the hostel with my colleagues, discussing the military forces that were now surrounding us. The atmosphere was oppressive; October 2016 was still fresh in our minds. I didn't know what to think anymore. I went to bed early, looking forward to the next day. I was supposed to be promoted and get a raise. Kirsten, my new American boss, had arranged everything. I planned on inviting our trainer Andrew to lunch at a good restaurant to celebrate.

At 3 a.m. I was woken up by a rumbling noise, the sound of projectiles whirling around before piercing someone's body. Shots were flying everywhere – to the south, north, east and west. Kneeling, I could see bullets exploding in the street outside the hostel through my window. I felt the vibrations through the walls. My legs were shaking, my knees too, making it difficult to maintain that position. Nevertheless, I stayed like that until dawn.

When I switched on my telephone, the news was out. ARSA – previously known as Harakah al-Yaqin – had once again attacked around thirty posts of the BGP. On X (previously Twitter), the group had confirmed its attacks. Immediately afterwards, the army chief, General Min Aung Hlaing, wrote on his Facebook page, 'The military and the police are fighting together against Bengali terrorists.'

On 28 August, the army began shooting at the roof of our hostel from their hiding place in a monastery across from us. We were forced to lie down on the floor to avoid the bullets and crawl to safety. We cling to life only when we are afraid. I was terrified. The authorities had decided to send the foreigners to Yangon for their safety. They left Maungdaw on the 30th. My colleagues, my friends, my brothers. As I hugged them for what would be the last time, I already knew that I would never see them again.

The sound of gunshots grew louder with each passing day and my life was in more danger than ever. My mother called to tell me that our village was burning. 'They are killing the men, raping the women. It has started again, my son. We have to leave.' She was crying, people were fleeing – it was all happening again. The following day, my parents decided to leave the country like the others. My mother kept calling me to join her, pleading, 'Son, I want to see you one last time before I die. I want to hold you in my arms.' I didn't even want to answer the phone anymore; the pain was too much to bear.

On 2 September, my brother who fled with them informed me that they had arrived in Bangladesh. They had managed to cross the border in a boat. The thing that I'd feared most had happened: now that they had left, my parents would never be able to return. There is no coming back from hell, after all. It absorbs you, crushes you. Even if you come out alive, deep within you are dead – the punishment is eternal.

In the centre of Maungdaw, the air had become unbreathable. The city roared like a volcano; belching out smoke, spewing torrents of flame that crushed everything in their path. Myo Thu Gyi was destroyed – not a single house was left standing – and the fire was spreading from village to village. From Noyapara to Dail Para, Hari Para to Maung Ni Para, and so on. I had to leave as soon as possible lest I perish.

My friend Hassan who worked with me at AAH had witnessed his house burning in front of his eyes. He had to bring his mother to our hostel to keep her safe. I hadn't seen him for a few days and when he knocked on my door, I couldn't recognize him. His cheeks were sunken, a few strands of grey hair had sprouted in his bushy beard, his hair fluttered on the top of his forehead. His shirt hung loose over his longyi and smelled of soot. Hassan held his mother in his arms, like a hurt child. She was weak and hungry. I ran into the kitchen looking for some leftover rice in one of the pots. I boiled water to brew black tea, mixing in a little condensed milk and sugar to balance the bitterness. His mother devoured it all while Hassan cried without pause.

'They killed my sister, my father, my brother, my son and wife. They came and burnt our houses. My sister wanted to leave. But as soon as she stepped out of the house, they shot her. She is dead! I couldn't even retrieve her body nor those of the other members of my family. Where is my wife? Where is my child? I will never see them again. I will not be able to give them a proper burial!'

Hassan couldn't finish his story. He kept talking about the funeral, haunted – he wanted a grave for his loved ones, a place where he could commune with himself. I didn't know what to say. I remembered his wedding that I had attended a few years before. Who could've imagined such a tragic ending?

'Take us to Bangladesh, we can't stay here anymore,' he finally said. 'Next time, they will come for us.'

'We will leave tomorrow morning, I promise you. Tell me, Hassan, who shot them? Who killed them, brother?'

'The soldiers.'

'How many were there?'

'More than a hundred. The Rakhines were helping them as well.'

It was exactly as I had thought. The soldiers had received orders to kill us. And the villagers, our neighbours, were their accomplices. My throat tightened, my legs trembled. I had to face the facts. This time around it was much worse, and I had to leave as soon as possible. That night, I tried to organize everything as best I could, memorizing the city map on my phone and the best route to the port. Hassan and I put together some money to pay the ferrymen. Every single note mattered. The deal was simple: pay the money, take the boat, cross the river and reach Bangladesh. But it was simple only in theory – many Rohingyas had been trapped.

I checked my bag one last time. I had instinctively packed my notebooks, pens, a few books, my computer, AAH business card and the receipt for my white card, my only identity document. It noted my date of birth, 3 April 1991, and called me a 'Bengali from Myanmar'. This was how they saw me, as a migrant who came illegally from Bangladesh. This was the only existence that they acknowledged. My card had been confiscated in 2014, but I had kept its receipt. It was proof that I was born in Myanmar and lived there, that I grew up breathing its air. This was all that was left of my life.

The following day, I set out with Hassan and his mother. Our goal was to reach the port of Maungni Para, the closest border to downtown Maungdaw, without being ambushed. I'd memorized the names of each and every road that we would have to take, and all the back roads in case Plan A didn't work out. The battalions could emerge at any moment. We started off by entering an alley but found a military truck parked right in the middle of it. So, we hid in an adjacent alley. I looked around me. The city was deserted, plundered and ravaged. They had once again erased every sign of life: the bustle of the markets, the eagerness of the shopkeepers trying to make a sale, the aroma of frying doughnuts and the bubbling excitement of children watching the spectacle.

The truck thankfully left before I lost my head. I knew that it was the last time I would see all this, the last time that I would walk on the soil of my country. My head was spinning. I just couldn't silence the voice inside me that kept saying, 'Don't leave, you will not come back.' I never wanted to leave my country but my choices were either to leave or die.

On the road, for the first time in my life, I saw two dead bodies. A young girl and an older man, their skin whitened by death. What had they done to deserve this? Were they the terrorists the authorities spoke about? It was too much; I collapsed on the ground and vomited. Several times. I could no longer stand the smell of blood and sulphur. After catching my breath, I wiped my mouth and the sweat on my forehead before pushing myself up on my arms. My heart was pounding – I could feel it in my chest and temples. My head was going to explode. Behind me, Hassan was crying. His mother had fallen down as well.

After a few hours of hide-and-seek with the police, we safely reached the small port of Maungni Para. It was the first time that I'd been there. We could see Bangladesh piercing the horizon in front of us. A dozen rowboats were waiting to cross the Naf. As the sun began to set over the river, one of the ferrymen approached us. 'It is 150,000 kyats per passenger!'

We only had 200,000 kyats in all. Hassan and I looked at each other, unsure of what to do.

'Son,' Hassan's mother called out to me, holding out her gold chain. 'Please give this to him.'

I hesitated; there were tears in my eyes. I didn't want her to give them anything – I wanted her to keep the chain. Hassan insisted. The piece of ornament that saved our life was a gift from his father, who had died many years ago.

'We have to wait till nightfall,' the ferryman told us.

'Why?'

'The Border Police post is nearby! They'll shoot if they see you crossing,' he snapped, visibly irritated by my naivety.

The people around me – about 100 others – were murmuring. I glanced at Hassan. He was pallid and his mother was dozing on his lap. I gave them a bottle of water and a little rice that I had brought along. Soon enough, the boatman signalled for us to get into the boat. We had to wade through the mud to reach it. The women were falling down, the men pulling them up like plows. I focused on trying not to fall. My pants were already heavy with dirt. There were fourteen of us in the little boat – men, women, children, babies. Two ferrymen were rowing on either side. The third was charting the course. We were packed tightly together; some clinging to each other as if their lives depended on it. Behind me, a boy was muttering to his father, 'Where are we going?'

'To Bangladesh.'

'Papa, what is Bangladesh?'

'It's a Muslim country. Don't worry and keep your eyes closed.'

I took one last look at my watch. 7:34 p.m. on 6 September 2017, my last minute in Myanmar. The monsoon wind was blowing something fierce and after a few minutes, the waves began to hit our boat, lifting it up and crashing it back down in sudden bursts. Frightened, the women chanted a verse from the Qur'an that Rohingyas usually recite when faced with danger: *'La illaha illa anta Subhanaka innee kuntu minath-thalimeen'* (There is no other God but you, Glory be to You! Indeed, I was among the wrongdoers). I was in the middle of a river that acted as a bridge between two worlds: one where I was stateless, and the other where I would become a refugee. In both cases, I had no place to call my own.

Under the moonlight, torches and human shadows finally appeared in the distance. We were arriving in Bangladesh. The boat ran aground and we had to jump knee-deep into the water. We were still a few metres away from the beach. The weakest passengers no longer had the strength to go any further. Exhausted by their flight, starving, they collapsed never to rise again. The seafoam quickly covered them like a shroud. This new land became a burial ground for their broken dreams.

I stood among them; looked at them. I was still breathing but I couldn't feel anything anymore. Water crashed against my feet and washed away the dirt that was stuck to my longyi – I didn't feel that either. My feet sank into the sand. I was frozen. Mute. Stock-still. Annihilated. The reality I was witnessing had surpassed me; it engulfed me like the backwash that had nearly destroyed our boat. How many of us were there on this shore? I was also a part of this tragedy.

'Born to suffer'

We crossed the Mayu Mountain.
We crossed the Naf river.
We crossed the ironed fences at border.
We cross the territory of death and dread.
We are born to escape for life
I escape as best I could.
The villages where I evacuate under attack soon.
Thundering sounds of gunfire rip through my ears
And the grave created for me is too wide.
There is a nail in my brain,
There is a dagger in my heart,
It is hurting, bleeding, cringing.
My lungs are suffocating.
May the Lord of Cruelty regret himself
This suffering is bottomless, no exit.
The fire, the water, the wind, the earth
Be at cost of our blood, flesh and skulls.
The organs of our body in two countries.
Some left their limbs behind in Myanmar
Bodies are carried to Bangladesh,
Others carried bullet embedded.

Frozen bodies, row on row,
Blue marble forms lying.
Not breathing, not dying
The bloom of evolving miseries.
Old men rely on bamboo sticks,
Women cling to life, clutching babies on their breasts
Grandparents in baskets hung by bamboo stick threads.
The shadow of hell on earth
Every night, I am killed
Every morning, I wake up again.
Each night, many men rape me
None listens when I sob.

14

First,
Burmese soldiers came to me,
Rabbed my land.
Second time,
They took away my money.
Third,
They burnt my home.
Next,
It is my soul.

– MAYYU ALI, 'Hunting for Souls'

WHAT WOULD BECOME OF us now? We had nothing left. Exile was not an end to our suffering. Instead, it was the beginning of a struggle, that of coming back from the dead.

With the rain and harsh winds, walking was a struggle. Our feet sank into the clay; some slipped and fell on the people next to them. Old men leaned on bamboo sticks;

sons carried their mothers on their shoulders and their children in wicker baskets. Exhausted, thirsty and hungry, we were nothing more than shadows of ourselves, reflected in the muddy waters. Once we got to the asphalt road leading to Teknaf, large trucks brought meagre supplies: bottles of mineral water, bananas and dry cake. How many days had it been since people had eaten? The crowd threw itself on the food packets; women fell down, children were crushed. Extreme situations unleash the innate tendencies of human beings – our basest instincts.

I waited in the distance for a bus that would take me to my parents. They were in the Kutupalong camp. Next to me, an old woman was moaning, holding her forehead in her hands – a sign of great sorrow in our culture. Everyone was looking at her. Terrified, I drew closer. She was sweating and trying to tie her batik around her waist. A thick, white headscarf covered her head. I tried to put her at ease. She held out her hands to me, trembling. Her son had been killed in front of her eyes by the military. They had entered her house and shot her son when he tried to escape. She and her husband had managed to flee, but at what cost? They would never be able to bury their son, who lay on the ground abandoned. How many bodies had they had to step over during the exodus?

I bought a Bangladeshi SIM card with the money that I had saved and used it to contact my brother, Sabar. Once the bus arrived, I copied the accent of a Bangladeshi man in front me to blend in while boarding. I chose to sit near the window to look at the landscape. Thousands of my people were wandering the roadsides, the edges of Bangladesh's wilderness. In the distance, I could see Myanmar, marked by columns of smoke in the sky. Maungdaw was still burning. My house was burning; the market, the school, my grandfather's lands. My entire life was burning before my eyes.

'This is terrible,' said a Bangladeshi passenger to his friend, who was sat next to me.

'How can the Burmese Army be so cruel?' came the reply.

After five hours, the driver rang the stop bell for Kutupalong. It looked like a veritable human anthill, there were so many people. I had never seen anything like it before. I crouched under people's arms and slipped in between baskets; a perilous exercise made worse by the slippery ground. Finally, I stumbled upon a tin sign that read 'Kutupalong Refugee Camp'.

When I looked beyond, the immensity of our disaster became clear. There were thousands and thousands of bodies lying on the ground – some on tarpaulins, most in the sticky mud. Emaciated, skeletal, lifeless bodies with vacant, evaporated eyes – already elsewhere, already lost. I didn't want to linger. I had to find my parents and most importantly, not think about all this. I wrote these words, long afterwards, about my feelings in that moment.

'The bang of immorality'
Quite ablazer than the flame
Sharper than a chisel
A blow of outbreaking mortality
Beyond the rise of immorality.

Immorality roams in human mind
Smashes out our conscience
And defeats the virtues ultimately
The last nerve of love then, roars up.

Cynicism comes by, ruffling the souls
Insanity upon kinship and friendship
The sign out of mercy and kindness
Hence, immeasurable wretchedness loads in life.

In the middle of the bang
The plight of hunger and thirst for new generation
A hive of ignominy for women nature
So the eclipse of human future.
The voyage of inaptitude strides up
No eyes can see the truth
Mouth can't speak of injustice
Hands can't save innocent lives.

I dialled my brother's number. He told me that my parents would be somewhere in the crowd and instructed me to go back up the main alley. Suddenly, someone grabbed hold of my arm. It was one of my neighbours from Boli Bazar, who led me to my parents.

As I slowly approached, I saw a body with bent legs on the floor, covered by a white veil. Was this person dead or alive? Close-by, a man wearing a soiled white cotton T-shirt was sitting on a plastic tarpaulin. My father. I ran to him, shouting, 'Papa, papa!' He tried to stand up with the help of his hands but was too weak – I had to hold him so he wouldn't fall. He looked at my face, touched my cheeks, nose, lips and shoulders with rough, damaged hands. In my chest, I felt my heart was being crushed. The frail figure next to him was my mother, at death's door. I sat down to hug her and she touched my face with her right hand. Shaking, coughing, feverish, my mother didn't even have the energy to smile.

'We walked for two days and one night to reach the border,' my father told me. 'It rained on the way. Everyone wanted to run as fast as possible to escape the bullets – it was every man for himself. Son, I was so afraid of dying.'

I looked at my mother. She too wanted to tell the story of her exile but couldn't summon the strength. I noticed dried mud on her feet, rising up to her knees.

How many times had she fallen during the journey? She suffered from chronic asthma and was diabetic; it was a wonder she had even managed to get here.

My cousins, nephews and nieces, neighbours, all were present in the crowd. I decided to return to the market to buy food – everyone could do with a little strengthening. On my way back, I met Sabar. His feet were still muddy and cold. He lowered his eyes, face darkened. He was avoiding my gaze. I took him in my arms. Soon, his son came to hug us. We were all crying. 'I've spotted a shelter next to the cemetery,' my brother told me. 'We have to hurry, otherwise we'll lose it.'

It was essential to find shelter before sunset, so we could sleep in safety and avoid exposing ourselves to rain and cold. My mother needed rest most of all. We hired two people to help us dig a plot and construct a tent using bamboo and tarpaulins. We had to exchange our kyats for takas to pay them. The rate quoted to us was 3,000 kyats less than the usual for 1,000 takas. It couldn't be helped – we needed the money to buy materials for constructing the tent and kitchen utensils for dinner: plastic plates, cups. Everything was temporary, just like the brittle ground. This was our first night together as refugees in Bangladesh.

My muscles ached, my feet were swollen. I struggled to keep my eyes open, no longer able to control my body.

Night had fallen but outside, people continued to walk, shout and look for shelter. Mothers raked the ground, levelling it so the children could sleep. Only those who had some money could afford to buy tarpaulins. Others slept in the open.

On 16 September, all AAH members received a message on the WhatsApp group that had been created to stay in touch and share important information. The organization wanted to take stock of those who had fled and those who had stayed. In Myanmar, I had been the one who used to help people. Now I was among the victims. There were 105 of us who had reached Bangladesh. That day I went to the local AAH headquarters and while I was leaving, some people stopped me. They introduced themselves as journalists from a French television station. I did a brief interview with them, narrating my journey. Later, some former colleagues who had long since returned to their homes in France sent me a screenshot. I had been on national television, on France 2.

I was a survivor. My parents were survivors. My brothers, sisters and cousins were survivors. All the people in the refugee camps were survivors. And in these camps, survival was an uphill battle. There was no electricity. We had to buy a solar panel to charge our phones and at night, we used low wattage lights inside the shelter. In the morning, people lined up to use the latrines. Everyone rushed to be first in line. Children defecated in the open; water tricked down and formed piles of refuse that attracted flies.

I felt suffocated. There were more than 200,000 refugees in an area no larger than one square kilometre. I had no space, no moments of solitude to write. I couldn't work and no longer had any savings to buy medicine for my parents. My headaches were getting worse, causing excruciating pain in the back of my skull. I had experienced violent headaches once before, during the 'cleansing operations'. But at that time, I could do relaxation exercises that I had learned during my AAH training. In the camps, I had no privacy. It all made me want to scream. But who would have heard my cries amidst hundreds of thousands of people wailing day and night?

My older sister lived with her husband and six children in a village a few kilometres away from the Ukhia refugee camps. I hadn't seen her since she left for Bangladesh in 1995. She invited me to stay with her, so one morning I travelled to her place. On the way, I came across a group of people who had just arrived in Bangladesh from Buthidaung. The journey took twelve days. We were joined by a girl, around fourteen or fifteen years old. She looked very young and fragile, and she held a little boy in her arms. Her clothes were in tatters.

She seemed to be looking for someone, so I went up to her. 'You can trust me. I am a Rohingya like you. I fled from Maungdaw a few days ago. I am staying in this village with my sister. Are you from Maungdaw or Buthidaung?'

'From Taung Bazaar in Buthidaung,' she said. 'My father and two of my brothers were killed by the soldiers. Only my brother and I were able to escape.'

'Where is your mother?'

'She died of an illness a long time ago.'

A neighbour who had helped the siblings escape came to talk to us. 'There are eighty-seven of us in this group. We are all from the same village. My son and son-in-law were also killed by the soldiers.' Some of the women no longer had veils covering their heads or shoulders; they wore simple batik. The children kept wrapping their arms around their mothers' thighs and tucking their heads under their clothes. The men carried their belongings. The entire group looked petrified, as if demons were still prowling around them.

A few days later, another French journalist texted me to ask if I could translate for him in the camps. With him, I went to the island of Shah Porir Dwip in Teknaf, the region where I had crossed the border. It was close to the Maungdaw city centre and hundreds of people continued to use that route to leave Myanmar. There, I acted as a translator for the first time, though I already had some experience from my work with AAH. The survivors said that they had been trapped by troops who had burnt their houses, raped the women and girls and murdered their families.

We met a woman who was carrying a basket on her hip and a child on her lap. When asked why she was leaving, she started screaming and fainted. I was able to calm her down, as I had been trained, by offering her water and explaining that she didn't have to speak to us if she didn't want to. But she wanted to – she *needed* to.

'Our village was burned down by the soldiers and Buddhist villagers. We hid in the neighbouring forest. We stayed there for four days. There was nothing to eat, so we gathered leaves and drank water from the ground like animals. Then we came down the hill and slept on a beach while waiting to get here. During the night, the army and the Rakhines abducted my husband and a few other men.'

Her husband was a fisherman. Together, they had three children. The young woman was clueless about what had happened to him until two Burmese journalists from *Reuters* – Wa Lone and Kyaw Soe – exposed the discovery of a mass grave in Inn Din in 2018. The reporters were detained for more than 500 days for abusing state secrets. The husband of this woman – with whom I have stayed in touch – was one of the ten victims massacred by the soldiers. There is a photograph of the persecuted kneeling, hands tied behind their backs like animals for slaughter, in front of armed men. It was widely circulated after the news broke. What had they done to merit such an execution?

For four days, I worked for the French TV channel. Each testimony we heard described crimes against humanity, mass massacres and systematic gang rapes. Everything pointed towards a genocide ordered by the head of the Burmese Army, with the tacit agreement of the government and its de facto leader, Aung San Suu Kyi. How could she authorize such horrors? The UN thereafter declared that the atrocities committed amounted to 'crimes against humanity, war crimes, ethnic cleansing, and bore the hallmarks of a genocide.' The word was officially out.

A few weeks later, Laura Haigh from Amnesty International called me. She wanted me to help her colleague, who was coming to Cox's Bazar to cover the exodus. Laura and I met in Maungdaw in 2015. I had helped her talk to a few Rohingya students who had faced discrimination from Buddhist teachers.

The following week, her colleague Matthew Wells arrived. He and I went to the border to conduct fresh interviews. One of the men we met was a native of Chut

Pyin in the district of Rathedaung, where hundreds of Rohingyas had been massacred on 28 August 2017. 'The military surrounded our village. Then they set fire to the houses. Some of them were shooting at us. Everyone was trying to run away; some fell down as they ran and were killed by the bullets. I escaped, but I had to leave my wife and children in the house. I could never return,' the forty-five-year-old sobbed.

I worked for two weeks with Matt at the border. He paid me well, enough to finally meet the needs of my parents. I liked working with him. However, I began to experience something strange: I felt overwhelmed. Whenever I tried to sleep, I remembered the words of the people we had met during the day. The bullets, the fire, the murders, the rapes – nightmares that robbed me of sleep. I spent the nights with my eyes open, imagining the scenes. My headaches started getting worse. After all, I was a survivor myself. I had felt death up close; I had also suffered trauma.

Sometimes I tried to go to the city centre of Cox's Bazar to enjoy the beach, known to be the longest in the world. It was an hour and a half away from the camps by bus. The Bangladeshi police had intensified their inspections since the crisis. Refugees were not authorized to go to the city but since I worked with the journalists, I sometimes climbed into their van to reach Cox's. But all I could think about were the massacres.

I received a growing number of requests from journalists, as those I'd worked with recommended me to their colleagues and friends. I took my work very seriously, since it allowed me to document the human rights violations my community had been subjected to. On one occasion, I went to a hospital near Cox's for a report, where they were treating injured Rohingyas. That day, there were about a dozen patients. Some had lost their legs, others their arms. Their limbs had been brought back by their brothers and sisters, while they crossed the border with battered, amputated bodies. I could hardly believe my eyes. One little girl could no longer move her body, after she was shot in the left leg. The eight-year-old wept as her father watched over her. 'My mother and I were at home. Suddenly, a bullet hit my leg. I fell down. I don't know what happened after. My mother was killed inside the house.'

All the injured people came from Maungdaw and Buthidaung. What they had endured was incurable – their stories were horrific, their experiences indescribable. How can one imagine the pain of walking for miles while bullets pierce one's flesh with every movement? That night, I couldn't sleep. The bullets of genocide do not spare even little girls.

Thousands of orphans lived in the camps. One day, with a journalist, I visited a dispensary in the Balukhali refugee camp. There were 115 children under sixteen years of age, reciting the Qur'an with a mullah. I noticed a boy who was frighteningly thin. He wasn't speaking, he remained still. I showed him to my colleague and introduced myself to him, wanting to gain his trust. The mullah came towards us. 'He lost his parents and siblings. He is from the Maungdaw district.'

'Which village is he from exactly?'

'He doesn't know.'

The boy was hardly five years old. He might have known his village once, but he'd forgotten everything due to the trauma. He was in dire need of help. I'd heard that DWB provided mental health support services. I encouraged the mullah to take the boy to the DWB clinic that was closest to the camp.

The more I worked with journalists – the more I dealt with the atrocities borne by my people – the more I suffered. I am also part of this tragedy. Journalists come and go; they move on to another subject. They are free to come back or forget about us. But I was in the midst of everything, trapped and unable to leave the camps.

One day, I returned to the camps to see my parents. I had been living in my sister's house for several months. It was a temporary arrangement, only till my headaches subsided, since she had very little space. The camps were evolving continuously; after the initial chaos, things were gradually being organized with near-military precision. Close to a million people were spread across thirty-three camps in the region, separated into small blocks. Each camp had a Bangladeshi political leader or camp-in-charge (CiC) and a Rohingya representative, the majhi. They were appointed by the Refugee Relief and Repatriation Commission, a Bangladesh government agency.

When I described my work with foreign journalists to my father, he told me that he had visited the Balukhali camp where most of our neighbours and my cousins were staying. He had met his friends and spent some pleasant moments with them. People from our village had opened tea shops and stalls in the alleys. My father wanted me to help him change camps. The very next day, I went there and found a shelter for my family. It was eight metres wide, quite enough space, and cost me 16,000 takas.

The relationship between the Rohingyas and the local population was very complex. They perceived us as refugees who had razed their forests to pitch our tents. I realized that here, too, we were bound to suffer the same discrimination. It was as though we could never be equal to another. In Myanmar, they called us Bengalis; here they called us '*Burmaya*', which meant Burmese.

One day, I took a rickshaw to my sister's place after working in the camps. Two Bangladeshi men were sat beside me. Suddenly, a Rohingya woman crossed the road in front of us, forcing the driver to stop abruptly. 'Fuck you Burmaya!' he shouted. They hadn't realized that I was a Rohingya too. 'Stupid Burmaya. Illiterate,' swore another passenger. Bangladeshis often mock the Rohingyas. '*Shaankir fuwa*, Burmaya' is the expression that I hear most often – son of a bitch, dirty Burmese.

Around this time, I also worked with a Norwegian journalist who had met Aung San Suu Kyi on many occasions. I told him about an open letter I had written on 14 October 2017 to The Lady in *Al Jazeera*. I held her responsible for these crimes, this exodus and our tragedies – even for burning my library. Here is an extract from that letter.

> Not only did you burn down my home, you burnt Nelson Mandela's *Long Walk to Freedom*. You burnt Mahatma Gandhi's autobiography. You burnt Leymah Gbowee's *Mighty Be Our Powers*. And you burnt your own book, *Freedom from Fear*.

Despite widespread international criticism, she has consistently denied these crimes. On 19 September 2017, in her first public address after the violence began, she stated, '[A]ll people living in Rakhine state have access to education and health care services without discrimination.' She posed with the military, the very people who had placed her under house arrest. It is because of her that there are more Rohingyas in Cox's Bazar than in Myanmar. Almost all human rights advocates and leaders of democracy have visited the refugee camps to observe our situation. Why hasn't she? What pains me the most is knowing that we were persecuted in the country of my childhood heroine, who will now forever be associated with our genocide.

15

I watched the blood streaming down
Where my husband and son were consumed.
Next, I watched
My baby thrown into the bonfire,
Burnt to fuel
Burnt to ashes,
Disappeared in the thin air.

– MAYYU ALI, 'Burning Alive'

SOME TRAGEDIES ARE WORSE than others, they haunt us more than others – so much so that it becomes difficult to transcribe them. Mumtaz Begum's account is one such story that will mark me for life.

A white bandage wrapped around her burnt face, some patches still bleeding. Another dressing around her right leg, pinned to the ground. She looked like a mummy. Next to her was a child who stared at me with wide, open eyes. I couldn't tell if the child was a boy or a girl, their head completely shaved and covered with a compress. The child was playing with plastic bottles that had been distributed by NGOs. Their shelter stood on a mound of earth that was about to crumble. There was practically nothing in the tiny room: a clay pot, some rice, a bottle of oil and two thin blankets.

The journalist I was working with that day wanted to interview women who were victims of massacres. One of my friends gave me Mumtaz's name with a word of caution, 'If you want to see the scars of genocide, all you have to do is look into her eyes.'

Mumtaz turned her torso slightly, while her legs remained still. The journalist and I sat in front of her to facilitate the conversation. We explained the subject of the interview and she agreed to speak. I made it clear to her that she could stop at any moment, that there was no obligation. I didn't want her to feel pressured by our questions. But like most survivors, she wanted to speak so that the world would hear and provide justice. Her voice was very low, prompting me to move closer so I could hear her clearly.

'I am from Tula Toli in Maungdaw. It started around eight in the morning. I was preparing a meal for my husband and children in the kitchen. Suddenly, I heard gunshots. I went out of the house to see what was happening. My neighbours were running. Children were crying. The hamlet was on fire.'

Mumtaz tried to get up, as if she wanted to describe and show something to us. But she couldn't manage it.

'I came back home and took my youngest child. My husband carried the other young one. We rushed with the crowd, both my older sons running behind us. We reached the riverbank. Nearly all the people of the village were there. We had to swim across the river but didn't know how. We needed sticks to do it.'

She bent down, scratching her face.

'It is so painful, it's unbearable – it hurts all the time. But I want to speak. A group of soldiers surrounded us on the shore. They started firing at us and beating the men and boys. Those who were left alive cried. Others collapsed, their chests hitting the ground. A heap of limbs – someone's neck, another's head, a leg. My husband and I were kneeling. The soldiers approached us and took my husband and two older sons. One of them pushed me. They started beating my husband and sons, until blood ran down their faces. My sons were quiet but my husband screamed with rage. They shot him, a bullet in the forehead.'

She burst into tears. My journalist friend gave her a small bottle of water. She helped Mumtaz drink from it, as her jaw was too sore to open her mouth properly. I couldn't believe what I heard; she was talking about the Purma river where I used to play as a child.

'They started taking the women to the centre of the village in groups. I didn't know what they were doing there. They kept coming back looking for others. A few soldiers started digging holes in the sand. They lit a fire and threw the dead into it. They dragged me away. I had my baby in my arms, held against my chest. One of them snatched my baby and flung it into the flames right in front of my eyes. I begged them to take it out of the fire. My daughter who is here with me today – she is all I have left – tried to rescue her brother. My baby! My baby! He disappeared. They dragged me and my daughter to the centre of the village and threw us on the floor of a house. There were five other women with us. First a soldier raped me and then another. Then two others raped me ...'

I lost control, unable to stop my tears from flowing. The journalist looked at me and whispered, 'It's horrible. I've never heard anything like this before, and I have reported on numerous conflicts across Africa, the Middle East and the Indian subcontinent.'

'I lost consciousness,' continued Mumtaz, her hand in mine. 'I began to feel hot – the temperature was rising, my body burning. There was a fire inside the house. My daughter tried to get me out, pulling me by my arms. She was bleeding. They had struck her head with a machete while I was unconscious. We spent the night in a rice field. The next day, my daughter and I walked into the forest. I had absolutely no idea where to go. We spent four days and four nights in the wilderness, eating leaves and drinking the water they contained.

'On the fifth day, I saw two other women – neighbours who had been raped like me. We began travelling together. We came across a group of Rohingyas who said they had come from Buthidaung. They told us they were going to Bangladesh and I decided to follow. After walking for two days, we reached the border. There were so many people waiting there. We had to pay to cross over but I had nothing, absolutely nothing. I cried, my face and leg burning. I couldn't walk with the injuries on my legs. I thought I was going to die. As night fell, two boatmen took pity on me and allowed me to cross with my daughter. When we reached the other side, we walked to a nearby village and wandered into the compound of a house. The family gave us something to eat and allowed us to sleep there. In the morning, they took us to the DWB clinic in Kutupalong in their car. I was treated there for fourteen days.'

It was difficult to visualize all that Mumtaz was saying. Every word she spoke felt like a knife being driven into my heart. How could a woman bear to watch her husband, two sons and neighbours being slaughtered in front of her? How can a human being burn a baby alive in front of its mother? How does one survive all this? Why was Mumtaz still alive after witnessing all this? Why? Why? What was the meaning of these massacres? The pain was too heavy to bear – how could one continue to live with such a burden?

After the interview, I told my journalist friend that I wanted to go home. I didn't have the strength to listen to any more tragedies. I was mentally exhausted and needed to rest. Mumtaz's voice echoed in my head. The scars of her burns, the open wounds on her body, the torn flesh under her clothes were all evidence of the genocide, of the atrocities that men are capable of. Those soldiers had wanted to eliminate her, destroy and traumatize her. What did the infant do to deserve to die in flames? What did the men do to have their throats slit and be butchered like animals? What did the women do to be defiled down to the deepest recesses of their beings?

I wrote a poem as a tribute to Mumtaz and titled it 'The Burning of Mumtaz'. She is the face of our tragedy. Her skin bears its scars. She had been burnt like my house, scorched like our lands. Like our rights, she had been violated and trampled upon. Her face will forever carry the marks of our people. But she survived. She came back from among the dead. Mumtaz is still here, with a desire to live. She is a survivor. The world must know her face, know her story. And with it, that of our people.

Like Mumtaz Begum, I interviewed dozens of rape victims who came from different villages. Thousands of Rohingya women and girls had been raped in the summer of 2017. It is impossible to get an exact number today, but the evidence is there for us to see. Later, I worked with a team from *BBC* to cover the Chut Pyin massacre, where we found that the military had systematically perpetrated rape. We interviewed Kushida, a thirty-six-year-old widow whose husband had been shot dead during the massacre. Here is her account.

> It happened in the morning. People started running after hearing gunfire. My husband and I came out of the house to see what was happening. There was fire and soldiers were chasing villagers. My husband and older daughter were running in front of me to escape the bullets. I followed them with my two other children, who were holding my hands. My husband was carrying our youngest daughter on his shoulders. Suddenly, my husband fell. I went to him. There was blood everywhere; he had been shot in the chest. I freed my daughter from his shoulders. And then, I don't know, a few seconds later, a crash of thunder tore through my ears. It was a bullet that hit my daughter's forehead. Blood was flowing down from her forehead, her nose, her lips, her neck. I lost my

husband and my daughter, who was in my arms. My children were crying. Behind us, all the houses were burning.

One woman pulled me up from the ground. I left the dead behind; I left my daughter and my husband. I had no choice. I grabbed my two other children and we ran till Ahtet Nan Yar, a neighbouring village. Soon a group of armed forces stopped us. We were eight women and four children. They took us towards the mountainside. I begged them to let us go. A soldier held me and dragged me behind a bush. There were around twelve of them. A few of them pointed their guns towards us while others lowered their pants. A pregnant woman screamed, holding her baby. One of the persecutors grabbed the child and tore it to pieces before our eyes. Why God? Why Allah, tell me why are we suffering all this? The mother screamed in horror; one of the men stopped her from helping her child. She fought him. Another man shot her at point blank range. She fell down.

We were all crying and wailing. I thought that they were going to kill me. My children were holding on to me. The soldiers pointed their weapons at us and spoke to us in Burmese but we couldn't understand what they were saying. They started raping us one after another. Three men raped me. I cried. My

> children kept looking at me – they did it in front of them. Oh Allah, protect my children. Then they left, like nothing had happened. Some were even whistling. My batik was soaked with blood. I took my children and went to the neighbouring village. I stayed there for two days. The following day, I joined the villagers who were fleeing like me. We spent two nights in the forest while crossing the Mayu mountains. After nine days, we reached the Bangladesh border. I gave away my gold earrings to pay for the crossing.

Kushida lost fourteen members of her family in the Chut Pyin massacre on 28 August 2017: her husband and daughter, her parents, four siblings and six cousins. The villagers said that the border police, the Burmese Army and some Rakhine villagers were involved in the killings. Today, it is believed that more than 400 villagers had been killed in Chut Pyin, while hundreds of women and girls had been raped.

Often, family members could not accept that their daughters had been raped, despite the trauma it caused. Many girls were disowned for being raped, which led others to lie about what they had experienced. This denial ate away at them. In April 2018, I collaborated once again with Amnesty International. This time, we were covering incidents of sexual violence. We had received information about a minor who had been raped by soldiers. This is what she told us when we met her:

> My father and brother escaped when the army entered our village. Four soldiers came into our house. Two of them took my mother away. The other two raped me. Then two more came inside and raped me again. I fell on the ground. I couldn't move anymore. Then my mother came and picked me up. I didn't want to tell her the truth, so I told her that they had beaten and slapped me and that I had fallen down. A few months later in the camp, I realized that I was pregnant. I hid it from my parents but when my belly got really big, my mother noticed it and I had to tell her the truth. I asked her to get it aborted, but she told me that it was too late. If I did it, I would die. The next day, she took me to the DWB clinic. The doctor told me that I was eight months pregnant. I didn't want this baby. I've lost my youth; my life is over.

A month later, I learned that the girl had delivered the baby in the DWB clinic and abandoned it. I heard other accounts too, of babies left in garbage bins or gutters. In the camps, women do not know how to carry out abortions and cannot calculate how far along they are.

They lack information and are isolated from others. Even though NGOs have tried to help these women, many among them do not have access to these services.

In June 2018, a team from Sky News called on me to help them document rape babies. This was one of the most complicated subjects I had dealt with – nobody wanted to speak about it and many women claimed they got pregnant by their husbands. Unlike other men, Senuwara's husband was understanding when his wife told him that she was pregnant.

'It is not her fault,' he replied when I asked for his thoughts. 'It's her destiny, her life. I don't care about what others say. A Rohingya imam in our camp told me to support her so I am doing my best to help her.'

During these interviews, it was important to guarantee the confidentiality of the couples and mothers. We assured them that their names would not be published and that their stories would be respected. This is why I have changed many names in my book. Before approaching a survivor, I first spoke to her husband or parents, only going forward with the interview when they agreed. But I also liked to ensure that the woman was willing to speak before proceeding.

'Oh brother, we've lost everything,' Senuwara told me. 'Soldiers surrounded our village. They started firing. Bullets were flying everywhere. The men and boys fled for fear of being killed. The women and children stayed at home. My husband escaped. My three children and I were trapped in the house. The soldiers came. They took away my two older children. I cried. A soldier snatched my baby and threw him to the ground with a lot of force. My baby was crushed before my eyes. Then four soldiers raped me.'

She burst into tears before continuing. 'I fainted. Then I heard a noise. Somebody was calling me – my husband, who had come back to look for me. But I couldn't get up. I begged Allah not to wake me up; I just wanted to die. My husband put me on his shoulders. He had to carry me all the way here – I had no strength left. After I arrived, my stomach hurt badly. I went to the DWB clinic many times and they gave me some medicine. But the pain continued until I could no longer sit down to pray. A few months later, I felt something in my belly. I understood that I was pregnant with a rape baby. I didn't want it. I wanted to abort it, but I didn't have the slightest idea how to go about it. In Myanmar there are traditional midwives, but here I didn't know anyone. One day, I decided to talk to my husband. He remained silent and didn't speak to me for two weeks. Then, little by little, he started talking to me and helping me around the house. Two months ago, I gave birth to the baby in the shelter.'

She was ashamed of being a rape survivor, a cursed

mother. 'During childbirth, I suddenly remembered the horror I had experienced. I kept having flashbacks of my rape. I cried and cried. Every time I look at the baby, I remember the horror. This is my son – he is innocent and I will never tell him all this.'

'Do you love him?'

'Yes, I love him. I love him like my other children.'

'And your husband, does he love him?'

'Sometimes he plays with him when he cries. I don't think he loves him like our other children.'

I felt she wanted to tell me something else. She did. She showed me her breast. 'Look at this mark. A soldier bit my breast while raping me.'

I hardly dared to look, not wanting to visualize her suffering. The bite was her scar of the genocide. 'Do you want to go back to Myanmar?'

'I will never go back. I don't ever want to see the house where I was raped and where my baby was crushed to death.'

According to data from UNHCR, out of a million Rohingya refugees, 52 per cent are women and girls. For many months, I interviewed women survivors of the Tula Toli massacre, the Monupara massacre, the Gu Dar Pyin massacre and the Chut Pyin massacre. The more interviews I conducted, the more I realized that women and girls had been the most brutally affected.

Many journalists and media outlets have documented their stories. Their suffering is featured on the covers of magazines and international websites. The reporters proudly hold up the awards they have won. But the crimes have gone unpunished. Is our genocide worth anything? How many more need to be killed? How many more women need to be raped before we obtain redressal?

'Crimes against humanity'

Not the scene of a Hollywood movie
Nor sequence of a bestselling fiction,
Gang-rape,
Slaughter,
Mass-grave,
Burning live.
The world is too brave to watch us being killed.
Burmese soldiers entered into my home, it was midnight
They took my father away, detained, tortured.
I went to see many times but never saw him again.
A Rohingya father is gone
A Rohingya is gone
No use of chemical weapons
Nor the blast of atom bombs
We are being killed one after the other

Not only by bullets but by the silence of the world, by the silence of the world.

As much as I heard of clatters of gunfire.
Bodies I saw fallen like leaves in the wind.
The killers enjoying the hunt.
I don't want to remember
but I can't forget ?

16

Our scream penetrates
into their offices.
Our blood gushes on the screen of conferences.
The more we die, the less the world cares,
World failed in the second genocide.

– MAYYU ALI, 'Voyage'

I'M LEFT FEELING BITTER. Who is fighting for us? To have our rights recognized, to represent our community, to make our voices heard? We are part of the media wave, but we are only the foam. No one really cares about what has caused the wave, what it is made of or what comes after. We are survivors, revenants from a world that no longer exists. To eat, to wash, to sleep – everything is a struggle. Mere survival does not leave room for battle. We can just about escape death – remain standing, not lose balance – like tightrope walkers who risk falling into the void at any moment.

At the break of dawn, men go to distribution points – often very far from their shelters – to receive food and basic necessities. Thousands of people queue in broad daylight under the scorching sun, some collapsing in the sweltering heat. Everybody wants to get back early but distribution takes hours, monitored closely by Bangladeshi soldiers who do not hesitate to strike those who break the queue. The line is long and straight. Each portion is measured. There are frequent fights – the people are hungry and sad to be in a country they have long feared. 'We had our own land in Myanmar,' they lament. 'We used to store food to last us from winter to the rainy season. Here, in the camps, we have to wait the entire day to get some aid. What misery!'

Under their makeshift tents, the women worry. Rumours run rampant, spreading troubling news. Aside from frequent kidnappings, there is human trafficking. Many victims are trapped by smugglers who sell them into modern slavery. Meanwhile, the children remain idle during the day. They are very young yet have lost their innocence. Some of them go to learning centres run by UNICEF and other NGOs, but they only offer reading programmes. Before sunset, fathers return with provisions on their shoulders. Mothers rush to cook. Families fall asleep on the floors of their shanties, vulnerable to the air and rain, wind and heat.

I didn't want to settle for such a life. One day in December 2017, I coincidentally met my old friend Mohib Ullah in the Kutupalong market. We had worked together for the AAH office in Maungdaw and had documented the crimes of the Burmese government while we were still in Myanmar. Mohib was a long-time advocate for our rights in Arakan. He had a serious air about him. He was a learned and eloquent man. His hair was always carefully styled with a side part. He liked wearing white shirts and black pleated trousers. He was so elegant that even in the camps, he had lost none of his grace and poise.

'*Boddah*,[3] what do you want to do for these people?' I asked him.

'We must form a team with young, educated and motivated people like you. A small team will suffice to begin with. Together, we will represent the people in the camps. We will make our voices heard and demand justice. I can no longer bear to stand by and watch people lament. We are going through a genocide. We must document this tragedy.'

Mohib had excellent political knowledge but didn't know how to engage the international community. No one here in Bangladesh knew how to go about it. 'Boddah, we would first need to get permission from the

---

[3] Older brother

relevant authorities in the camps to organize meetings. Do you know the Rohingyas who have been living here for a long time? They can help explain the steps we will need to take.'

A few days later, we invited several men to one of our shelters – long-term refugees, teachers and religious leaders. We were fourteen people in all, of whom I was the youngest. We needed to know more about the living conditions of the refugees. Some had been registered by the UN as refugees of Kutupalong and Noyapara since 1993. There had been just under 300,000 refugees before our massive influx of close to 740,000 people.

'Is there a social network in the camp?' I wondered.

'There are a few. But none are very active,' replied Abdul Shukur, one of the registered refugees. Unlike the new arrivals, he had been recognized as a refugee by the UNHCR.

'So how do you manage things?'

'Some are working for children's education. Others are helping to improve the condition of women in the community.'

'Do you have permission to work?'

'Yes, we obtain written permission, signed by the CiC. One day, for example, we asked him to allow us to take videos of traditional songs, inspired by our life in Myanmar. He agreed.'

And so, the movement was launched. With some help, we obtained permits, expanded our network and created a central committee. There were twenty-six of us at the next meeting, fifty at the one after that. Word of mouth worked well for us, enough that we could begin the real work. Some wanted us to first call on Myanmar to restore our rights, others wanted the UN to register us all as refugees. But I was sure this wouldn't be effective. 'We must collect evidence, proof of our genocide. Many people in the Western world still do not know exactly how many Rohingyas have been killed, raped and reported missing. If we want justice to be done, we first need proof.' They all agreed with me.

We decided to organize ourselves by forming teams in each of the main camps: Kutupalong, Balukhali and Thaingkhali. Each team would collect testimonies. To be effective, we made a questionnaire with clear and concise questions: the number of houses burned, the number of people killed, raped or missing. We then cross-checked the information village-wise to get an idea of the extent of the massacres.

This is how I was able to obtain more information on the Tula Toli village. We identified approximately 500 deaths among the 4,000 residents of the village. Evidence was provided that men from the 33rd and 39th battalions – known to be the most dreaded in Myanmar –

had carried out the attacks. Some villagers said that they saw Burmese Army helicopters hovering in the sky the day before and on the day of the killings. The Muslim neighbourhood was razed to the ground, while that of the Buddhists remained untouched by violence. The Burmese were killing us with impunity while sparing their own. We had to find more proof to build a case for the International Criminal Court (ICC).

Two months later, each team presented information on villages in the three townships of Maungdaw, Buthidaung and Rathedaung. We had reliable data on the victims of each type of crime, but we had to keep going. In June 2018, I was hired by Fortify Rights. I could hardly make any time for the network. Mohib managed the teams all by himself, though I often spoke to him on the telephone and visited him whenever I could.

Over the course of time, the organization grew. Mohib even had his own office in Kutupalong in a long bamboo shed. Neatly hung on the wall were the words 'Arakan Rohingya Society for Peace and Human Rights' (ARSPH) and on the door, 'We Demand Justice'. Mohib Ullah had also listed the demands of the Rohingyas on a large placard:

- Deploy UN security forces in Arakan prior to repatriation
- Consult with UN leaders for repatriation talks

- Put an end to illegal accusations against the Rohingyas in Myanmar
- Administratively restore the ethnicity and nationality of the Rohingyas
- End the genocide against the Rohingyas and bring the perpetrators to justice
- Give equal rights to the Rohingyas like all the other ethnic groups in Myanmar
- Compensate for our losses in Myanmar
- Ensure the safety of our lives in Myanmar, our country

All these demands were addressed to the Burmese government, to guarantee our safe return. Sitting on a plastic chair in the middle of that room, Mohib resumed his past activities. He was the president of the association – the only one that represented our interests from Bangladesh. He was in direct contact with foreign delegations, diplomats and human rights advocates who came to visit the camps. He was even invited to the White House in the summer of 2019 for a meeting with Donald Trump, to talk about minority communities. Whether in Kutupalong or the Oval Office, his message remained the same: 'I want justice to be done, for us to return home and to be considered as citizens of our country.' Mohib Ullah would be assassinated a few years later at the association headquarters on 29 September

2021, after receiving numerous death threats from armed gangs. Our community lost its greatest leader, and I lost one of my best friends.

17

All I want, is to see pens and books
In the hands of Rohingya youths
Instead of knives and guns.
I want them to choose literature
Instead of extremism
I want them to write for cohesion and reconciliation.

– MAYYU ALI, 'Writing for peace'

WHILE WORKING FOR FORTIFY Rights, a realization struck me: nothing was being done for the youth. The learning centres run by UNICEF were no longer sufficient. Ten years earlier, in my village, I had started an education programme with a few of my friends during our summer vacation. We wanted to explain the school curriculum in the Rohingya language because many students did not understand their teachers' language. More than 1,000 students participated. We asked for only 200 kyats as an admission fee from the students and held the programme on the grounds of our village mosque. The initiative was so successful that it was replicated in many other villages in the region.

In the camps, there were many teachers among the refugees who had lost their jobs in exile. I wanted to mobilize them. Together, we could once again make education accessible for our youth. When I told the teachers about my plan, they immediately agreed and even proposed that we buy a shelter as quickly as possible to hold our first class. For this, we would need 20,000 takas or roughly 345,000 kyats. After many calculations, we estimated that we could start four classes with approximately twenty students each. This would require us to buy four shelters in our Balukhali camp. I could buy two, but not more. I had to provide for my family. We had to find another solution. So why not the mosque? We decided to meet the imam to discuss the project, who offered us a space inside the mosque in our block.

But we also needed authorization to open schools. The majhi, who worked in close collaboration with the administrative head of our camp, offered to accompany us to see him. The in-charge was particularly interested in what we were going to teach, since Rohingya students were not allowed to study the Bangladeshi curriculum in the camps. I reassured him, stating several times that we would only teach the Burmese curriculum. Satisfied, he gave us permission.

We decided to start classes on 1 July 2018. I requested all the teachers to spread the word in the camps. The children had already missed more than a year of school, so we had to make up for lost time as quickly as possible. To do this, we made a timetable, with a final exam scheduled three months later. Never before had education seemed so important to me. It would offer new perspectives to these young people whose horizons, until now, had only been crowded with an endless expanse of tarpaulins and makeshift tents.

I constantly think about ways to rebuild our community. Several educated Rohingyas have fled to Europe, Malaysia, Indonesia, Thailand and more. They are actively advocating for our cause before the UN and the entire Western world. Though this work is important, very few are interested in strengthening our community in Myanmar and Bangladesh, as if they have forgotten that our problems began with the destruction of our people. We have been destroyed, erased, subjugated, punished, wounded and killed. We first need to be resurrected.

I wanted to empower the young men and women of our community. To build a civilized society where everyone would be able to read and write, where women – who were all too often victims of domestic violence – would be respected. We lived in a patriarchal society, and it was imperative to change that. We needed to raise awareness about gender equality, personal care and hygiene, and about peace and reconciliation.

I had many ideas, but I needed help to materialize them. I wanted the advice of some of my former AAH colleagues who were now working in the camps. So, one Friday, I organized a discussion workshop with the theme 'Rebuilding the Community' at our new school in Balukhali camp. Twenty-two people made the trip, however, I couldn't help but feel disappointed. Two female colleagues I really wanted to involve in our project were unable to attend.

I explained to everyone why reconstructing our community was of utmost importance, focusing especially on the needs of our mothers, aunts, daughters and so on. I decided to give a piece of paper to each participant. They had thirty minutes to propose suggestions. They brainstormed in groups while I went around the room to listen to them discreetly. Before ending the workshop, I emphasized on children's education, youth empowerment and raising awareness about the problems faced by women and the elderly. Some participants wanted to ensure that the latter were not forgotten, because they too contribute to the development of our society.

I took the opportunity to announce the creation of our Community Rebuilding Centre (CRC) and request their support. We needed equipment: benches, whiteboards, plastic chairs and tables. Within a few minutes, we were guaranteed all the supplies we required. We also had to offer the teachers some remuneration, otherwise they wouldn't be able to invest adequate time in the project. I suggested 10,000 takas per month, the same salary as a job in an NGO. If we offered any less, they would prefer to work elsewhere. Finally, we agreed on charging a small fee to parents who could afford it. This would allow us to begin classes on 1 July with enough time to see things through.

As planned, we started classes on 1 July. I visited one classroom on the first day. Inside, there were fifty-three students, including six female students. About a dozen more were standing outside because there wasn't enough space for everyone. It was very hot under the tarpaulin roof. Hamid, the teacher, had taken off his shirt. The students were sweating.

'Assalamu alaykum,' I greeted them. 'My name is Mayyu Ali. I am a teacher. I came here today to see all of you. Tell your parents that the Burmese curriculum books are available in the new markets. Please ask them to buy them for you. And please attend classes regularly, it is important.'

That evening, I called on all the teachers to take stock of the situation. I told them, 'We need to limit the size of our classes. We cannot accept more than fifty students per class, otherwise it's not productive.' The programme was formally launched and we created our Facebook page, CRC-Education, where we regularly posted information about our classes and the courses offered. In December 2018, after we received funds from a friend abroad, the teachers could be paid in the long-term. In January 2019, we opened a new school in the Kutupalong camp. We hired six teachers. This is the largest school in the camps that offers the official Burmese curriculum. It has 800 students.

Proud as I was, I did not want to stop there. The young people were not yet independent. Empowered young people can serve as excellent pillars of a civilized, socially and culturally developed society. I wanted to instill confidence and teach them to be self-sufficient. Me and a few friends started three training courses on thinking skills, peace, reconciliation and inclusive writing. We offered these courses in three different centres with the help of our friends. We estimated that close to 300 young people could benefit from them every month.

I gradually discovered that the young Rohingyas wanted to write but were afraid to start. This made me smile. I remembered myself, in my room lit by an oil lamp, fearing that my mother would discover my notebooks. Some of them had sent messages to me because they couldn't muster the courage to speak to me face-to-face about their desire to write. A few had brilliant ideas but didn't know how to put them into words. I encouraged them by making them do exercises to develop their imagination and style. I also gave them tips that I used myself, like 'Read as much as possible and write down everything you learn.'

Art saved us – it liberated and unchained us. When we wrote, we could leave the camps behind and imagine another life; we could sail on an ocean of hope, light-hearted and released from the burdens of the past. We could be leaders, politicians, business leaders, football players. Writing presented a world of possibilities. We simply had to let ourselves get carried away by the flow of words – without worrying, without intellectualizing. Simply free to imagine what we dreamed of being.

Our daily lives are so violent that we need a lot of imagination to survive. Women and children are targets of trafficking and kidnappings, taken away to be sold as prostitutes in Cox's Bazar, Chittagong, Dhaka and sometimes even Kathmandu and Kolkata. They are rendered sex slaves devoid of names, faces or stories, mere pieces of flesh that are exploited to the bone. Some say that prostitution exists even within the camps.

Often the traffickers approach desperate parents and offer to take their children to better homes in Cox's Bazaar, where life is simpler and food more plentiful. Hoping for a better future for their young ones, they accept. I once met a woman who gave away her five-year-old daughter to a Bangladeshi couple. Supposedly, she was meant to do their housework but I don't dare imagine the truth. On the other hand, some parents want to marry off their daughters – one less mouth to feed. Smugglers manage to convince them to send the girls to Malaysia or Indonesia, where Rohingyas living clandestine lives buy them at cheap rates.

One day, I met a mother whose daughter was a victim of trafficking. Here is her testimony:

> My daughter was in touch with two Bangladeshi women who wore the hijab and burkha. They pretended to work for NGOs. One of them told me that her parents in Chittagong were in need of a housemaid to help them cook. They could pay her 2,000 takas per month. My husband was killed in Myanmar during the violence. I fled with my four daughters. I am alone, I don't have the money to feed them. So, I gave my daughter to these Bangladeshi women. For two weeks, my daughter called me from Chittagong. Then she disappeared. I never heard from

her again. I lost my daughter because I am poor. I don't have anything.

I've heard such stories countless times.

Another scourge was eating away at the camps: the rise of radicalism. Men from ARSA were forcing young people to join them and take up arms with the objective of returning to Myanmar. They were spreading terror among the Rohingya refugees.

Akbaar is a friend from my village in Myanmar. He had been in love with a girl since primary school and after they both fled to Bangladesh in August 2017, Akbaar wanted to marry her. The marriage was nearly fixed, but another man also wanted to marry this woman. He spoke about this to his friends and the news eventually reached members of ARSA. The leaders convinced him to join the group. In exchange, they promised to do everything they could to get the young woman to marry him. Not long after, this man and his new comrades arrived at the woman's shelter at night and forced her to marry him.

Instead of knives and machetes, I advised young people to pick up pens and open books; to choose knowledge and literature over extremism, art over war. Towards the end of October 2018, I published my first poetry collection, *The Blossom*. It comprised of all the texts that I had published in Burmese magazines before the violence of 2012. I printed 1,000 copies and distributed them amongst young Rohingyas, especially in the CRC schools. Through this book, I wanted to convey that education was the only solution. When faced with ignorance, stupidity and wickedness, education and culture would always be the best protection.

I saw that the youth also enjoyed reading my poems on social media, so I wanted to create an online platform to expand their knowledge. The idea was to allow them to write whatever they wanted. I identified twenty young people who I felt best expressed their feelings and emotions and contacted them directly on Facebook. In March 2019, I invited all of them to a poetry workshop at one of our centres. But there still weren't any women among the participants, which saddened me. After the introductions, I asked them to tell me why they wrote. 'I write to cope', 'I write to express my emotions and my feelings', 'I write to tell my story to the world', they revealed. Though their motivations varied, I could sense the sincerity of their words. I, too, wanted to share my perspective with them.

'We Rohingyas have our own art and culture. Due to exile and suffering, we've forgotten them. Creation and writing are acts of resistance against those who want to wipe out our culture and destroy our people. The moment has come to revitalize our art. The entire world needs to recognize us, not only because of our unfortunate circumstances but also for the beauty of our culture. Let us revive it together!'

They were so enthusiastic. We started the first workshop with a lesson on figures of speech followed by writing exercises, including poetry. On 21 March, World Poetry Day, we launched a Facebook page where all young Rohingyas could post poems, quotations, essays or articles. With the input of several friends, we chose our name: The Art Garden Rohingya.

On the very first day that we launched the page, we had 6,000 fans, some of whom were not Rohingyas. Today we have more than 300 poets who write for us, including nine women. This has been my greatest source of pride. We have published over 1,000 poems in both Burmese and English, though most young people prefer the latter so they can reach the whole world. Their poems speak about the pain, trauma and persecution faced by our people in Myanmar. Very few write about love, romance or nature.

Here is an excerpt from my favourite poem written by Jahangir Alom, one of the young poets.

'Question Marks'
No helping verbs,
in the sentence of my life-journey.

If there's something,
That's none other than,
Question mark and question mark
With thousands of question marks,
I'm still breathing, still alive,
Living my life, like a student,
Always in the examination hall.

We published our community's first anthology under the aegis of editors James Byrne and Shehzar Doja in 2019, titled *I am a Rohingya.* It is the result of our solidarity and collective work. I finally felt that I'd bequeathed something to the future generation, as if I'd fulfilled my destiny – to pass on our culture.

18

Seeing beauty of your feature
I believe the existence of paradise

– MAYYU ALI, 'The one'

MY PARENTS ALWAYS WANTED me to marry young. By 2018, I was the only unmarried person in our family. In Arakan, Rohingya parents think that marrying off their daughters or finding wives for their sons is their principal responsibility. They must attend all their children's weddings before they die. They often speed things up; even more when there is a hefty dowry. A good marriage is believed to be equivalent to a dowry of 1,000,000 kyats, a motorcycle and furniture. Those who do not have the means are often unable to marry off their daughters, so they accept any man – the first one who agrees – regardless of whether he is poor, illiterate, drinks or loses too much money gambling. Since the parents of the bride pay for the wedding in our culture, what matters most is having one less mouth to feed. The worst part is that most do not see the faces of their future spouses, with whom they are supposed to spend the rest of their lives. It is forbidden to meet before the engagement. All my sisters got married this way in Arakan.

One night, after I went back to the camps, my mother woke me up in the shelter. '*Fuut*,[4] your father says that he likes Nooru's daughter.' I was still asleep, but I knew what she was doing. My father had sent her to convince me to marry this girl I'd never heard of before. 'They are from the same village as us. Your father is friends with hers. She is educated; she'll understand you.'

I remained silent. My father, who slept in the next room, had never discussed marriage with me but would often send my mother or my brother's wife to ask me if I wanted to get married. I was adamant that I would not marry until my future was secure. Surviving alone here was hard enough. I did not want to be a bad father to my future children – I wanted to give them a peaceful and secure life, whether in Myanmar or elsewhere, but never in Bangladesh. To be born in these camps was a punishment.

'Fuut, if I die before you are married, I won't be able to rest in peace,' cried my mother. Her words made me

[4] My son

sad, and they echoed what she had said to me before the 2017 violence. Everyone spoke to me about marriage – my aunts, my uncles, my parents' friends. Whenever they visited our shelter, they'd say, 'So you're still not married, what are you waiting for? Your parents are sad that you are single; they're worried about you. They are old and could die soon. Get married, let them celebrate your wedding before they die. Your mother wants to see the face of her future daughter-in-law.'

I am very sensitive and they knew it. Hence, this emotional blackmail usually worked on me and made me think about my parents worrying about my marriage. I could not understand this traditional perception of marriage – I wanted to marry someone I loved, someone I knew. There's no way I'd let someone else choose for me. But it was also unsettling to think I might be a cause of worry to my parents.

In Myanmar my reply was simple. 'I don't want to get married. I need more time.' But here, I could see my parents ageing faster. They were seventy years old. My father suffered from high blood pressure and congestive heart failure; my mother was diabetic, asthmatic and had contracted hepatitis in the camps. She began experiencing dizzy spells like my father. I was worried about them, afraid of losing them. I wanted them to be safe before they died; I did not want to bury them in Bangladesh. I wanted to see them free, surrounded by their children and grandchildren, for the first time in their lives. That would be a beautiful day – that was my dream for them.

All my principles vanished the day I met Shanas, a young Rohingya woman who had been living in Bangladesh for several years. Prior to the escalating unrest, some Rohingyas had managed to settle in this country by passing themselves off as Bangladeshi. I worked with Shanas's sister. One day, she invited me to her house – a rented apartment she shared with her family. That's where I met Shanas for the first time. She smiled at me constantly. She was short, much smaller than her sister, with long, ebony hair that covered her back and piercing black eyes that were full of life. I immediately felt at ease with her, as though we already knew each other. She was beautiful, talented, intelligent. But most importantly, she was fearless.

'What do you want to do once you finish your studies?'

'I want to work for the emancipation of girls and women, to empower them,' she replied confidently.

I could see the passion in her eyes. She seemed so sure of herself. It was the first time I had met a woman with such confidence, as though nothing could stop her from achieving her dreams. I was impressed. When I got home that evening, I wrote my first poem about falling in love, 'The One'.

When I saw you for the first time,
My heart smelt down,
Seeing beauty of your feature
I believe the existence of paradise,
Looking at your eyes
I see the angel.

It is a strange moment when you realize that you have met the right person, the one with whom you will share the rest of your life. She, like me, wanted to help our community. I couldn't have dreamed of a better spouse. She alone could understand me and help me achieve my goals. Only she accepted that I was willing to risk my life to help my people. And little did I know then how much …

We got married on 17 December 2018, to the great joy of my parents, in a small, private ceremony to avoid raising any suspicions.

Like me, Shanas enjoys writing. She has already posted five poems on The Art Garden Rohingya. Here is one of them:

'My first day at school'
In that morning,
I was so exciting.

Too early I went to school,
To find a front seat at classroom.

My heart was filled with joy,
When I found the first seat in classroom
'This is not for kalar,' Sayama told me.
She sent me back and I was shredded.

That day, she taught me something (discrimination)
Not from curriculum but from her ill heart.
Me who went to school smiling,
And came back home crying

I love her so much.

19

Is this poison or death ?
I cannot name.
Is this the earth or the hell ?
I cannot differentiate.

– MAYYU ALI, 'A living hell'

MOST OF MY WORK around this time was doing research for Fortify Rights, an organization with which I collaborate even today. I conducted numerous studies on human rights violations with them. My colleague Noor and I managed a team of four Rohingya men and four Rohingya women. We called it the Rohingya Research Team. Noor led one group and I another. Every participant had to respond to this list of questions:

- Tell us about your background in Myanmar.
- Do you feel effects of chronic stress due to the exile?
- Have you been a victim of human rights violations in the camps?

- Have you experienced a traumatic event?
- Do you experience symptoms of trauma in the camps?
- Do you experience depression or anxiety?
- What are your activities of daily living in the camps?
- What is your opinion on ARSA?
- How do you feel about returning to Myanmar?

We even translated this questionnaire into the Rohingya dialect. What first struck us was the fear that the participants felt when responding to the question regarding ARSA. 'There are ARSA members in each camp. We will be tortured and killed if they find out that we are talking about them,' a person told us on the condition of anonymity.

We completed our survey in August 2018, having interviewed 495 Rohingyas across thirty-three refugee camps. These investigations into the mental health of the refugees were necessary to ensure that our trauma and tragedy were acknowledged. Our team identified several cases of depression and suicidal thoughts; among them was a man named Abdul Rashid.

Abdul had contemplated killing himself after he witnessed his old parents and two brothers being shot dead by soldiers in Long Don, close to my village. He was brutally tortured by the same soldiers but managed to escape. Every night since arriving at the camps, Abdul had the same nightmare, of his family getting killed. 'I can't stand these images anymore. I want to die, please let me leave this earth.' The fifty-five-year-old man had very dark skin, drooping eyelids and a long beard that he had apparently stopped trimming a long time ago. 'I have tried to hang myself twice since I came here. Unfortunately, my son saved me.' I put him in touch with the DWB team that managed a psychological support programme. The following week, he'd already had two sessions at their clinic.

A nineteen-year-old woman named Tosminara also told us she had considered suicide. She hailed from northern Buthidaung and had been raped by the Burmese troops. She fell pregnant but decided to opt for an abortion in a clinic. Her parents were too old to take care of her and her two younger siblings, so she was tasked with looking after them. They lived in the Balukhali camp. She told us, 'I didn't want to get married but my parents forced me to marry a man. Every time I sleep with him at night, I am reminded of how much I suffered when I was raped in Myanmar. I was raped by three soldiers. I still feel the pain inside. I want to kill myself.'

Every person who participated in our survey suffered from either depression or anxiety. In the camps, an estimated 75 per cent of the population suffer from serious psychological problems. Some fear that they will be forced to return to Myanmar with no guarantee of their rights and safety; others fear that they will live in the camps forever. Two months after the survey, we went back to visit all the participants and share the results. They were happy to see that we were concerned about them and hadn't forgotten about them. Though many of the refugees had been interviewed earlier, there had been no actual follow-through. They had lost hope, not knowing what had become of the testimonies and quotes they had given for articles and reports.

After this assignment, I became a human rights consultant for Fortify Rights. It was a source of pride for my parents. As part of my work, I investigated rapes. The testimonies were all appalling, and I also discovered a new issue: male rape. One of the people who agreed to answer our questions told us, 'First, they undressed me. Then they burned my penis with a lighter and sexually abused me.' Another man said that he had been unable to sit down since arriving in the camps. 'One wouldn't imagine doing this even to a dog.' Still others said that they were 'too ashamed to give an account of what happened'.

I also helped prepare a report on the ARSA situation in the camps. Certain members of the armed group had managed to cross the border. It was difficult to ascertain precisely what they wanted to achieve. Perhaps they wanted to lead an armed conflict in Myanmar to restore our rights, but the details remained unclear. What the report did demonstrate, however, were the threats, torture and abductions of Rohingyas committed by the armed group. Two Rohingya women humanitarian workers said that they had been abducted along with their families because of the work they were doing. Here is a testimony from one of them:

> I was taken to a mountain top far away from my neighbourhood by an unidentified person, to a makeshift mosque. I cried all the way. Once I reached the mosque, I saw my husband and many other men being tortured. They were being kicked and punched. One of the men said to me: 'Can you see how we torture the men? If you work, you will suffer the same fate.' I resigned for fear of reprisal.

In some areas, ARSA made their own rules and acted as morality police, bending the laws of Islam. If its members saw a woman talking to a man, they would threaten her. They reproached women humanitarians for working, which is not in our tradition. According to another testimony, death threats were frequent. 'At a meeting in a refugee camp in early 2019, a few Rohingya men who identified themselves as ARSA representatives told us that we had to make monthly payments to them. They declared: "You have to support us. If you go against us then we will kill you."'

The director of Fortify Rights, Matthew Smith, launched the report on 14 March 2019 with the declaration, 'When Rohingya militants abduct, torture, and threaten Rohingya civilians, they mirror the Myanmar Army ... Perpetrators of these crimes should be held accountable in fair and impartial trials.'

In working for Fortify Rights, I became a target because I denounced the acts of violence committed by the armed group. After all, as a peace activist who always chose to pick up the pen rather than the gun, I couldn't sit back and do nothing.

A few days after the report was announced, I began receiving threats. ARSA members called my brother's friend and said that they wanted to meet me, which I refused. I learned that my photograph was being circulated in their WhatsApp groups. They had sent it out to many people in the camps with the intention of finding me. Two or three days later, I was informed that an ARSA leader wanted to meet me in person. My superiors supported me as much as possible. Every day, a new and more influential leader would express the desire to meet me. I grew increasingly worried, especially with the escalating number of reported murders. I decided to leave the camps permanently – it had become far too dangerous for me.

On 27 March 2019, in a cafe run by a Rohingya in the Jamtoli camp, a few young Rohingya men were drinking tea with a friend of mine. Beside them sat a mullah and two ARSA members. They first talked about Mohib Ullah, who had recently traveled to the UN headquarters in Geneva to discuss our situation on behalf of ARSPH. Then the conversation turned to the publication of the report.

The mullah asked, 'Do you know this Mayyu Ali? He is the one who wrote the report. He is the Fortify Rights representative in Cox's Bazar. He is betraying our community by publishing a report on ARSA.'

'Are you sure? I don't think that association has any staff living in the camps. How could Mayyu Ali know all this?' someone retorted.

'Fortify Rights recruited him. He follows their instructions.'

'But how can he hold such a position?'

'I don't know. All I know is that he works for them.'

There were rumours about me everywhere; I could feel the noose tightening around my neck. Finally, they abducted my brother to question why I refused to meet them. They threatened to kill me if I didn't stop working. Fortunately, they released my brother after two hours without hurting him. I was terrified. Some people knew that I had left the camps. If they revealed this to members of ARSA, they could hurt Shanas or me. On 1 April, we decided to relocate for our security. I didn't reveal my location to anyone, not even to my parents. I was worried that ARSA might abduct them as well.

We rented an apartment with the help of a friend. In this place where I didn't know anyone, everything seemed new to me. Being a Rohingya was already a daily struggle; being an activist now put the fear of death in me. I was living in hiding, experiencing the same fear as when I would see soldiers as a child. I hardly ever left the apartment, except to go to the mosque. My wife bought fish and vegetables for us. She did everything for me, for my peace of mind. I knew that Shanas was scared too but she didn't show it. She was only nineteen, yet so much stronger than me.

I never went back to the camps and haven't seen my parents since. It's like I entered another world. Even though I continued to work for Fortify Rights by conducting interviews over the phone, I led a clandestine existence, cut off from the rest of the world. All my life, I've been surrounded by people – my grandfather loved to entertain. It all seems like a lifetime ago … More than anything, I felt useless. I knew that the youth were in desperate need of help, but I could no longer meet with them.

Despite everything, I never put down my pen. I still write. Writing is my weapon. My friend Pramudith Rupasinghe, who is also a writer, has been a constant support. I met him for the first time in the AAH offices in Maungdaw. At the time, I didn't know who he was. One of my colleagues introduced him to me as a famous writer, after which I read some portions of his bestselling novel *Bayan* online. As a Rohingya, I could not open a bank account in Myanmar and was unable to buy the book. I feel tremendously fortunate to have met Pramudith in one of the most inhospitable places on the planet. It was like discovering a river in the desert. I told him that I was an admirer of his work and that I, too, was a writer. 'One day, one way or another, our paths will cross again,' he said as we parted.

While in exile, I sent him a few of my poems, seeking a publisher to take them on. He wanted my book to be released through his own publishing house, Black Raven. He told me, 'No poet is born to fall, Mayyu.'

In June 2019, I published *Exodus: Between Genocide and Me*, a small book of twenty poems. This collection depicts the pain, sorrow and vicissitudes of the Rohingyas. My verses portray the tribulations and losses suffered by my people during the treacherous journey across the Mayu mountain range, the barbed wires of the barbarians at the border and the weeping Naf river. Seeing my book published internationally, I felt like I had given birth to my first baby. Here is one of the poems from the collection.

'No place on earth'
Once I was born, survived in different worlds,
One where I have lived for generations,
Another where I am merely a refugee,
In both places, I have displaced.
Terrified eyes,
Emaciated bodies,
God only knows how many days they have not eaten
They are afraid of eating what they find,
Because they will be hungry again when it's finished.

The publication of *Exodus* helped to build a bridge between me and other Burmese poets. I read my poems for the first time at an event in Yangon in July 2019, virtually. I was invited by Maung Saungkha, an eminent Burmese artist who had been imprisoned for six months in late 2015 for writing a poem entitled 'Image' which contains the following lines: 'I have the portrait of the President tattooed on my manhood. My wife is utterly gutted.' By inviting me to the gathering, he made a clear and unequivocal statement about his beliefs: freedom of expression and interfaith solidarity. It was a great risk for the organizers, for even the word 'Rohingya' is banned in my country.

When I said *mingalaba*[5] to greet the crowd, who were able to see my face thanks to a video projector, I felt like a Burmese once again – still alive and connected to my country despite being a refugee. In the colonial era, famous Burmese poets began writing about British rule and the need to fight for independence. It was through this art form that they conveyed messages and encouraged the people. Under the junta, poets have tried to talk about the political situation indirectly. Now I had the opportunity to do multiple readings of my poems, some even in the presence of the Rakhine poet Won Roe. It was quite symbolic.

Thanks to poetry, my words transcended borders. I was confined to my apartment but I knew that elsewhere, someone was reading my verses. My words could even enter the offices of my oppressors – they could travel above the walls placed between our two communities. Words do not have a religion. They are tools that I will use to reconcile both our communities.

But relief is always temporary. When 200,000 Rohingya refugees gathered in the camps for the second

---

[5] Good day

anniversary of the 25 August exodus, the government of Bangladesh disconnected 3G and 4G networks in the area. They accused some NGOs of helping the Rohingyas organize the events.

Not long before, the repatriation of many families to Myanmar had failed, like it had been failing since the beginning of the crisis. No one wanted to be repatriated without security, and the government was forcing us to accept the National Verification Card, the sole condition of our return. This card is proof of our erasure; it deprives us of our rights and makes us foreigners in our own land. We no longer want that. We want to and must be recognized for who we are, Burmese citizens.

After the demonstrations, Mohib Ullah became a target because he was one of the main organizers. He was threatened and refused medical care when he was sick. After being forced to live in hiding for many weeks, he returned to the camps but he never stopped receiving threats from the Bangladeshi government and from ARSA, like me.

New restrictions were imposed, making it forbidden to sell SIM cards to Rohingyas or employ us. The Rohingyas now have very limited means of communication in the camps. At night, people are afraid of being abducted by gangs and there are frequent robberies. Movement is restricted; we can no longer go from one camp to another.

We feel constricted. On 2 December, the Bangladeshi authorities began installing barbed wire fences around the camps. Rohingya refugees are going to live in open-air prisons, like the ones in Myanmar.

The Bangladeshi police have also started hunting Rohingyas living outside the camps. Rohingyas are arrested and villages raided every day. On 21 September 2019, the Bangladesh police arrested twenty-four Rohingyas in Chittagong and imprisoned them. On 2 October, they arrested and detained forty-five Rohingyas from a house south of Chattogram. Thousands of Rohingyas have been living here for many years now; some have even managed to obtain Bangladeshi identity cards. This is considered a crime today. Arrests have been made in several universities. Rahima Akter, a Rohingya student of law at Cox's Bazar International University, wasn't permitted to attend classes because someone reported her.

When they're not threatening to forcefully deport us to Myanmar, the Bangladeshi authorities pressure us to transfer to Bhasan Char, a remote island prone to flooding, where they have already constructed infrastructure resembling concentration camps. No one wants to go there. One of the men who was forcibly put on the departure list said to me, 'I can see the trees of my village from here, it still feels like Myanmar. I would rather they kill me than be sent there, where we will all drown and die.' The camps have become a powder keg, ready to explode at the slightest spark. I have a feeling that this is going to end badly.

Today, my fear is twofold: being killed by ARSA or thrown into prison by the Bangladeshi police. I furnished my Fortify Rights identity card to rent an apartment. At home, we never speak Rohingya, only Bangla. I am trying to learn it – my wife gives me lessons so I can lose my accent. I avoid the Bangladeshi families in our building. I don't want to build any connections; I do not want them to suspect anything. We tell everyone that we are Bangladeshi because the locals hate the Rohingyas. They are likely to call the police the moment they see one of us anywhere other than the camps. We hide our language, our identity, our customs, who we really are. This is the only way we can survive.

20

Perpetrators lie in various ways.
While the world still debates on genocide
You can see the fire but not how we are burnt,
You can read of killings but
Not how throats were cut.

– MAYYU ALI, 'Genocide'

12 DECEMBER 2019 MARKED a new chapter in our history. On that day, Aung San Suu Kyi testified in defence of Myanmar in the International Court of Justice (ICJ). On behalf of the fifty-seven Muslim member-countries of the Organisation of Islamic Cooperation, Gambia accused my country of genocide against the Rohingyas. The public hearings began three days earlier with the words of Gambia's Minister of Justice, Abubacarr Marie Tambadou: 'Why is the world standing by and allowing such horrors again in our lifetime? … it is not only the State of Myanmar which is on trial here! It is our collective humanity that is being put on trial.'

For the first time in my life, our suffering is being acknowledged. The world has looked the other way for a long time, not wanting to see our tragedy, hear our cries or be held responsible for its inaction. Yet doing nothing means letting things happen. To say nothing, to not oppose something, to stay neutral is to become an accomplice to the worst horrors; to passively collaborate in crimes.

Today, the entire world is watching these hearings – from Gambia to Bangladesh, the refugee camps to the pagodas in Yangon, the Oval Office to the ICJ. They are listening to the arguments that are ushering in a turning point in our history. No one can now say 'I didn't know'. The world ought to know.

Over the last few decades, there have been a growing number of reports denouncing the crimes against our community. In November 2017, the Asia Director of HRW, Brad Adams, declared, 'The military's grave crimes committed with impunity are exactly what the International Criminal Court was created for. The UN Security Council should refer Burma to the ICC, but until that happens UN member states should ensure investigations take place and evidence is preserved for future criminal proceedings. If the Burmese military continues to operate with impunity, we are likely to see future rounds of violence against the Rohingya.'

In July 2018, in a report entitled 'They Gave Them Long Swords', Fortify Rights described the extensive, thorough and systematic preparations for genocide and mass atrocities against the Rohingyas in the weeks leading up to the attacks of 25 August 2017. The report details several points, as follows:

- Systematically 'disarmed' Rohingya civilians, confiscating household items that might be used as weapons or in self-defense
- Systematically tore down fencing and other structures around Rohingya homes, providing the military with a greater line-of-sight on civilians
- Trained and armed local non-Rohingya communities in northern Rakhine State
- Suspended humanitarian aid and access to Rohingya, systematically weakening the civilian population and removing monitors on the ground
- Enforced a discriminatory Muslim-only curfew in northern Rakhine State and evacuated thousands of non-Rohingya citizens from the area
- Built up an unusually sizable military presence, incommensurate with the threats at hand

Another report, from the UN fact-finding mission, was published on 16 September and cited at length by Gambia during the ICJ hearings. The UN clearly speaks of genocide in the report and demonstrates that Myanmar was motivated by 'genocidal intent'. It also states that 'there is a serious risk that genocidal actions may occur or recur, and that Myanmar is failing in its obligation to prevent genocide, to investigate genocide and to enact effective legislation criminalizing and punishing genocide.' More specifically, the mission highlighted 'seven indicators from which it inferred genocidal intent to destroy the Rohingya people as such, all based on the consideration of indicators of genocidal intent in international case law':

> first, the Tatmadaw's extreme brutality during its attacks on the Rohinyga [sic]; second, the organized nature of the Tatmadaw's destruction; third, the enormity and nature of the sexual violence perpetrated against women and girls during the 'clearances operations'; fourth, the insulting, derogatory, racist and exclusionary utterances of Myanmar officials and others prior, during and after the 'clearance operations'; fifth, the existence of discriminatory plans and policies, such as the Citizenship Law and the NVC process, as well as the Government's efforts to clear, raze, confiscate and build on land in a manner that sought to change the demographic

> and ethnic composition of Rakhine State, the goal being to reduce the proportion of Rohingya; sixth, the Government's tolerance for public rhetoric of hatred and contempt for the Rohingya; and seventh, the State's failure to investigate and prosecute gross violations of international human rights law and serious violations of international humanitarian law, both as they were occurring and after they occurred

The world cannot say now that it didn't know. How can anyone today deny our genocide? Sitting in front of my computer, hidden in my squalid apartment under the threat of death, I see my country Myanmar defending itself.

To William Schabas, the renowned advocate who agreed to defend Myanmar and stated that '10,000 deaths out of a population of well over one million might suggest something other than an intent to physically destroy the group', I would like to say: Come and talk to these mothers, these orphaned children, these fathers who have lost one of their own – tell them it is nothing. I want to remind you of your interview with *Al Jazeera* in 2013 for the documentary *The Hidden Genocide*, in which you said, 'When you see measures preventing births, trying to deny the identity of the people, hoping to see that they really are eventually, that they no longer exist;

denying their history, denying the legitimacy of their right to live where they live, these are all warning signs that mean it's not frivolous to envisage the use of the term genocide.'

To Aung San Suu Kyi, who sat with her head down – weary, impassive – for three days, assuring the court without the slightest doubt that 'genocidal intent cannot be the only hypothesis', I would like to say: What happened? You were my childhood hero. What happened to the person who said in 2012 that

> Rape is used in my country as a weapon against those who only want to live in peace, who only want to assert their basic human rights. Especially in the areas of ethnic nationalities, rape is rife. It is used as a weapon by armed forces to intimidate the ethnic nationalities and to divide our country. This is how I see it: every case of rape divides our country. Every case of rape divides our country between peoples, between genders, between the armed forces and ordinary citizens, between ethnic nationalities, so we must do everything we can to put an end to this.

I want to tell you, Madam Aung San Suu Kyi, that it is time to stop looking the other way. Come to the camps, meet Mumtaz Begum, look at the scars that have abraded half of her face and try to tell her that she made it all up, as you so want to make everyone believe. How many more women like Mumtaz have to be raped to break your silence?

To Min Aung Hlaing, the head of the Burmese army, who was conspicuously absent from the hearings and wrote on his since-deleted Facebook page that '[t] he Bengali problem was a long-standing one which has become an unfinished job ... The government in office is taking great care in solving the problem', I want to say that we are only people after all, like you. We belong to the same country, we breathe the same air. What could have turned you into this heartless being that ordered our destruction?

To all the executioners, oppressors, soldiers, racists, rapists, murderers – those who have erased our culture and destroyed our lives, those who silently let it happen – I declare: Read my poem and become cognizant of the horrors you have caused. You might want to erase the evidence, but this poem will remain forever etched in your memory.

'Genocide'

Perpetrators lie in various ways.
While the world still debates on genocide
You can see the fire but not how we are burnt,

You can read of killings but not how throats were cut.
They grabbed our land and built units and prisons,
And there, they detain and torture us
They took our properties and bought weapons
And they murder and kill us.
I was gang raped, set alight and left for dead,
I carry the scars of genocide inside my body.
The documentation of my suffering offered prizes
But my pain hasn't earned the justice yet.

For years, I watched Buddhists insist that their race was superior, sacred and pure. We were likened to the 'fast-breeding African cichlid', to 'an invasive species', to maggots. In several immigration offices, I saw this refrain: 'The earth will not swallow one race to extinction but another race will'. It was a reminder to the immigration officers that they needed to be extra careful when issuing identity cards to Rohingyas and other Muslims in the country. This slogan became the basis of the anti-Muslim campaign which was later taken up by extremist monks. People were taught that we were the enemy and that is what we became, without even doing anything. This is how our genocide began in Myanmar. When will we find peace?

Today, 600,000 Rohingyas still live in Arakan and are at risk of further acts of genocide. Today, my Arakan has been razed to the ground. I can no longer see mosques rising in the sky, I cannot see my grandfather's lands, I can no longer see the mango tree in his garden. But they can never take away my pen – my words will be swifter than their bullets. Despite enduring the worst tragedies, I have seen resilience in the eyes of women and courage in the eyes of men. Voices are rising for our freedom, for justice, for reparation. I have fought and will continue to fight for the revival of our obliterated culture.

21

I want to fly to the sky of freedom.
I want to grab some peace.
This is the hope that helps me to survive.

– MAYYU ALI, 'Freedom'

WE HAVE ALREADY ENDURED so much and now, in 2020, we are facing a pandemic which has claimed millions of lives all over the world. My friends from the West are experiencing what we have been going through for so long – being deprived of liberty – but the comparison stops there. Their confinement is due to a virus, ours the hatred of others. They are gradually returning to their former lives, while ours don't exist anymore.

I am not afraid of this virus, and neither are my people. I am scared of its implications. Since the first Covid-19 case in the camps was officially announced on 14 May, authorities have restricted access to NGOs, though we depend on their aid to survive. Rohingyas can no longer work and don't have enough income to buy the supplies needed to avoid the spread of the virus, like protective masks and soap. Dozens of people share the same water pump and latrines. Hygiene is a luxury. Social distancing is a utopian idea in an area where the average population density fluctuates between 40,000 and 70,000 people per square kilometre. WHO is training young Rohingya volunteers to reach out to their communities and teach them preventive measures, however, these efforts are far from sufficient. Markets have been closed, food rations distributed by the few associations that continue their work are dwindling and many fear the likelihood of a famine.

The Internet is usually down and there are many who are completely unaware of the pandemic. Due to lack of information, wild rumours about the coronavirus are spreading – for instance, that those who contract the virus will be shot dead. People who fall ill are thus afraid to go to the camp clinics, even though UN agencies are building facilities to isolate the sick. The testimonies reaching me from those who have sought out medical care are distressing. 'The doctors discriminate against us,' a forty-year-old man named Reyazul Karim, who lives in Kutupalong with his wife and six children, described.

> I have been suffering from Hepatitis C since I left Myanmar. The treatment is so expensive that I cannot afford it, since I don't have a job. On 9 April, I went to the Gonoshasthaya Kendra (GK) clinic in Camp 4 at 10 a.m. from Kutupalong. The doctor was a Bangladeshi. I asked him for permission to enter his office. He refused outright and started shouting at me, 'Don't talk to me, leave! You [refugees] are dirty people.' I asked him to examine me because I was feeling very sick. He didn't want to listen and shouted once again, 'Don't come near me, leave, you may be infected with the virus, and you will transmit it to me!' I wanted to reassure him by telling him that I had a mask, that I was a hygienic person, I washed my hands, that I was an imam but he didn't want to hear a word of what I said. He yelled at me yet again and asked me to leave.

It is difficult to ascertain the consequences of this pandemic in the camps. How can one know for sure? Tests aren't being conducted. It is impossible to count the victims amongst us. Many young people have died suddenly in the last few months. Is it due to coronavirus? Or is it due to the exhaustion of an arduous life? Friends from my village who were otherwise healthy have died overnight. Omar Faruk, an interpreter, was barely twenty-one. He died in the refugee camp where he'd lived all his life, overworked by the daily task of collecting and transmitting information to the international media. How many more Omars will we have on our hands? How many broken lives?

Tragedy recurs month after month. Every monsoon we are hit by terrible floods. Tens of thousands lose what little they own: tents, clothes, kitchen utensils. These people have nothing left and must rebuild everything once again. A genocide, a virus, natural catastrophes … how many more nightmares must we endure? How many more lives will be lost? The more we die, the less people seem to care. The Rohingya spirit is strong. We will continue to struggle for our rights in Myanmar and Bangladesh. However, this is not possible without international help.

The situation is even worse in Myanmar. Arakan is cut off from the rest of the world and there is almost no internet access in the north of the country. Fighting between the Burmese Army and the Arakan Army, an independence group, has intensified since the beginning of the year, displacing thousands of people. After the hearings in December, the ICJ ordered preventive measures to be taken in Myanmar to avoid a new genocide. But soldiers continue to kill innocent civilians with impunity, Muslims and Buddhists in Arakan and Christians in the north.

In response to this situation, Amnesty International swung into action last July, by reiterating 'its call for the UN Security Council to refer the situation in the country to the International Criminal Court'. They also stated, 'Until there is genuine accountability for those responsible for crimes under international law, there is little hope for improvement in the lives of ethnic minorities in Myanmar.'

Sometimes I catch a glimpse of light through this fog. It always comes from poetry. In July, the Poetry Book Society based in the UK awarded the inaugural World Choice Honour to our first collection, *I am a Rohingya*. This is the first international award that was conferred to our literary movement. It is not just an honour but also an encouragement to all those who, like me, are trying to revive our culture.

The glimmer of hope always vanishes as quickly as it appears. In the month of November, I began receiving many phone calls from leaders of ARSA. The calls have grown increasingly intense. They have been inviting me to attend a meeting they are organizing in the camps with various Rohingya leaders. I know they are lying, trying to intimidate me and find out where I am. If they manage to find me, what will they do? Kill me? Rape my wife?

They abducted my brother once again; beat him, extorted money from him and threatened to kill him if he spoke to anyone. My brother is afraid. He writes to me, asking me to save him, but I can do nothing. Unable to leave this apartment, it is as if I am pinned to the ground.

I have more and more trouble sleeping. I have survived the violence, a genocide; lived in the biggest refugee camp in the world, hungry and thirsty; mourned the deaths of my brothers and sisters. Yet living a clandestine life is by far the worst thing that has ever happened to me. I have been deprived of everything, and I feel that I am going crazy. My wife often tells me, 'It's difficult for me. How much longer must we lie and hide who we are – hide our identity?'

All of this has been eating away at me – I can no longer protect her. I know that she hides her fears from me, to preserve my sanity. She is young but so strong that it surprises me every time. She's been my biggest pillar of strength as I face these obstacles. She believes in me, so I will have faith for the sake of my wife. I force myself to remain positive. This is the most important virtue for a survivor like me. But sometimes I can't stand being away from my family. In those moments, I think of returning to Myanmar just to get the feeling of being at home again – to touch the soil, to smell it. To be in my house and see my mother cooking, my father returning from fishing. I fall asleep at night imagining all this, knowing that it is impossible. Everything has been burned down to the ground.

22

This coup is the hunter of peace
The murderer of democracy.
They bow their lord and wait for a command,
They can hunt anyone, anytime and anywhere

– MAYYU ALI, 'The Coup'

MY COUNTRY IS TEETERING on the edge of an abyss. My sister called me in the early morning of 1 February 2021 to tell me, her voice weak and worried, that the military had seized control of Myanmar during the night. She was worried about her husband and three children and didn't know who to turn to for help. Aung San Suu Kyi had been arrested. The army generals had cited electoral fraud during the November 2020 elections as a pretext to their actions. The National League for Democracy had emerged triumphant, winning 82 per cent of the seats and bettering their 2015 results. I saw this landslide victory as a betrayal. It seemed like the Burmese people were condoning the massacres committed against my people, the complicity of the Lady from Yangon and the impunity of the army. How was this possible?

Aung San Suu Kyi was supposed to be sworn in at the end of January but on the 26th, General Min Aung Hlaing openly contested the results and called for a verification of the electoral rolls. On 30 January, the army denied that they were planning a coup d'état amidst myriad rumours. Some believed the military propaganda, but they were mistaken. We should never trust someone with blood on their hands.

Those who gave the order to kill the Rohingyas one by one now seized control of our motherland. Our executioners took the helm of my country as I watched on, incredulous. On my computer screen, I could see military tanks parading through the empty streets of Naypyidaw, Mandalay and Yangon. With their roaring machines, soldiers took over every alley, pointing their guns at those they were supposed to defend.

Soon enough, the Burmese people reacted. Protest demonstrations were organized in the biggest towns of the country. Doctors, teachers, students, workers – everyone gathered in the streets to say 'no' to the junta and a civil disobedience movement was launched. To counter the guns of the military, protestors displayed flags in the name of freedom, democracy and justice. I read in several newspapers that women had joined the front lines of the movement, their longyis acting as flags of resistance. They hung them on electrical wires to deter military officers from entering their neighbourhoods, since an old tradition maintains that any man who passes under clothes worn on the lower part of a woman's body will lose his virility.

Women also became the earliest martyrs. Mya Thwate Thwate Khaing was the first victim on the long list. This young Burmese woman, twenty years of age, was fatally shot in the head during a protest march in Naypyidaw. Victims fell as soon as they were shot. Young Kyal Sin became another symbol of repression. This nineteen-year-old woman was wearing a T-shirt that read 'Everything will be OK' when she was killed by a bullet in the head by the Burmese security forces during a rally in Mandalay. Even children were not spared. Khin Myo Chit, a seven-year-old girl, was fatally shot while sitting on her father's lap.

I feel powerless languishing in my apartment. So, I continue my work, collecting testimonies with NGOs and journalists. They all recount horrors: abductions, shootings, intimidation, violence, beatings, blood and more death. Everything we've already experienced; everything the Burmese people have long preferred to ignore.

Men and women, young and old, Buddhists, Christians, Muslims – the army shoots at everything that moves. Regardless of the reprisals, the Burmese youth are ready to do anything to avoid living under the rule of the junta. It is courageous, fair and admirable. For a long time, I feared for my people; today, I fear for every Burmese person. For the first time in our history, the people seem to be united. Messages of solidarity are being exchanged between communities. In the Kachin State, in the north of the country, a nun poses with a Muslim woman and a Buddhist woman. In demonstrations, there are banners addressed to the Rohingyas. Some express regret: 'We regret not believing you', 'We are with you', 'The army must be held accountable!' I never thought I would see this in my lifetime.

People are finally waking up. We are no longer 'kalars' or 'terrorists', but human beings. In the camps in Bangladesh, all Rohingyas support the civil disobedience movement – their only hope of returning to Myanmar. Few feel compassion for Aung San Suu Kyi. It is difficult to forget that she supported our executioners in The Hague. She disappointed me so much that I, too, find it difficult to feel sorry for her. I do not want to harbour feelings of anger or a desire for revenge, but I will never understand how she could compromise herself to this extent. She should have been a symbol of national unity;

instead she became the face of our genocide. I wonder if she will spend the rest of her life in detention …

Before this coup, hatred had taken root in the hearts of the Burmese people. Now, they have been delivered from it and seem to understand that the army is our one and only enemy. They divided us, now we must fight against them. I can't help but remember my dear grandfather, who told me about the first coup d'état in 1962, when General Ne Win seized power. It might seem that history eternally repeats itself, but I do not believe in destiny. Our unity will free us, I am sure of that. Myanmar will one day be a democracy, not this sham democracy that some wanted to convince us of in 2015.

Poetry has always been a clarion call for revolution in my country. Words can heal the wounds caused by weapons; verses call for courage and resistance. Before dying in detention in May 2021, the poet Khet Thi wrote these words:

I do not want to be a hero,
I do not want to be a martyr.
I do not want to be a coward,
I do not want to be stupid,
I do not want to be the one who allows injustice …
If I have only a minute to live,
I wish to have a clear conscience.

And also,
They shoot in the head,
But they do not know
That revolution
Dwells in the heart.

Khet Thi's body was returned to his wife with several organs missing. More than thirty poets have been imprisoned by the junta since the 1 February coup, and many others are in danger. Some amongst them still write secretly. One anonymous Burmese poet said, 'There are so many crimes against humanity [in Myanmar] ... Our poems and our verses are hordes of screaming children.' Their pens bleed, and so does mine.

'Bleeding Pen'
I write a poem
On skulls
I write a poem on skulls,
On bones and
On teeth,
I write a poem in tears
In blood and
In dying breaths,
My pen is bleeding
Poetry is mourning

But I will keep on writing.
One day I shall write a new poem
In laughter
In victory
In freedom.

For some, however, words no longer suffice. My friend Maung Saungkha, who read poetry with me at an event in Yangon in 2019, has decided to take up arms and join the defence forces. He continues to write and post messages on social media from the jungles where he is being trained. In a photo that he recently tweeted he looked extremely different; very thin. Why did a man who always advocated for non-violence join an armed group? Why are Burmese youth joining these groups? What do they want? The answer is simple. Freedom. Freedom to live. Freedom to speak. Freedom to write. They are ready to do whatever it takes, even lose their lives.

Seven months after the coup, on 1 September 2021, the Assistance Association for Political Prisoners (AAPP) reported 1,041 deaths, 7,742 people arrested and 6,107 people currently detained or convicted. Myanmar is in agony. When the Burmese people are not being imprisoned or killed by the military, they are dying of Covid. There is a shortage of oxygen support; hospitals are closed; corpses litter the streets due to lack of space in mass graves. The coup d'état has ruined the public health system. How did my beautiful country descend into such horror? It has been given a double sentence: a pandemic and a dictator. Pain divided us for a long time, now it unites us. My country needs freedom like human beings need oxygen. The international community, once again, looks at us and says nothing. Meanwhile in Arakan, more than ever, the Rohingyas are the most forgotten of the forgotten.

'The Waves'
The water of the Ayeyarwady is longing for
Its companion, the breeze.
The river is searching for the shore.
As long as its currents are flowing,
We'll keep clutching, clawing, and striving.
As long as the waves are roaring,
We'll keep rising, growing stronger.
This is the beginning of
'The third wave of the struggle'
To recover Myanmar's peace
To save 'Our Golden Land' once more.

23

For the first time,
When I behold her
I see the God's finest art,
She is soft like a rosebud
She smells of heaven.

– MAYYU ALI, 'First Sight at Inayah'

IT'S NOW BEEN FOUR years since I arrived in Bangladesh. I had thought that I would stay here for a few days, maybe a few weeks, then go back home. It's as though I wanted to convince myself to believe it. While leaving Arakan, I had looked around earnestly to ensure that I forgot nothing. I wanted to remember every detail, every colour, every smell, before they disappeared while I was away. On 7 September 2017, my heart was burnt, just like my house which had been reduced to ashes. No matter how hard I tried I couldn't bring it back to life. I felt dead inside. Until one day, 3 June 2020.

During breakfast, my wife was looking at me differently. It was the first time that I had seen her like that. At last, she said, 'Darling, I have to tell you something … I think I am pregnant.'

I was petrified. I had always refused to have a child in this terrible situation.

'Alhamdulillah!' I exclaimed and held her in my arms. All of a sudden, the fear disappeared. 'You know, I also have something to tell you. I had a dream last night. I dreamt that we had a little girl who held a treasure inside her. People were trying to catch us. It was a strange dream but finally, one morning, the three of us set out on a journey before the demons could get to us. And we managed to find a safe place where we could watch our princess grow up.'

Shanas smiled at me. She often makes fun of my flowery side. We went to the clinic for her to take a pregnancy test, and it came back positive. We couldn't stop jumping for joy! For the first time we forgot our fear of being discovered, of being noticed. Nothing could be more beautiful than our unborn baby.

On 26 February 2021 – a few weeks after the coup – our daughter Inayah was born. Inayah means 'gift of God'. I wrote these few lines right after I saw her.

'First Sight of Inayah'
For the first time when I behold her
I see the God's finest art,
She is soft like a rosebud
She smells of heaven.

A few weeks later, she inspired me to write this verse:
'Inayah Growing'
To watch you growing is such magical,
You're the wine of beauty,
The divine in paradise
You're the best poem ever I write.

The birth of my daughter gave me the greatest happiness, but it was also a moment of intense anguish. I could not share this experience with my loved ones, like all new parents do. My mother could not hold her granddaughter in her arms. For almost two years we had been living in hiding; alone, isolated from everything, facing only ourselves with no possible future in sight. I no longer had the strength to carry on. Sometimes I would break down. I counted the days, waiting for something, someone who could make it possible for us to leave this abyss and regain some semblance of humanity.

Due to the threats I had been subjected to, I applied for asylum in 2019 from the UNHCR. Canada agreed to receive us, the government gave its go-ahead and Amnesty International began preparing our file. We waited two years for the phone call that would allow us to leave. Two ycars of being told that our departure was imminent; of packing our things only to realize our travel had been cancelled the day before. The idea of leaving everything terrified me; I had to be careful not to leave anything behind. Every call felt like an electric shock running through my body: a surge of hope, followed by the fall. Every time I had to start believing all over again – in a better future, that I too would have the right to be a free man one day. What had I done to deserve to be locked up like this?

Now that our daughter was with us, we did not want to wait any longer. I did not want her to experience fear, insecurity or insult. I was often fearful before her birth, and now my anxieties had increased tenfold. On 2 August 2021, a UNHCR agent called me to say she had some good news. 'The government of Bangladesh has no objection to your going to Canada.' I put the call on speaker so that my wife could hear her words. Tears rolled down Shanas's cheeks, tears she'd been holding back for two ycars. I knew that it had been difficult for her; at twenty-one years old, she'd had to leave her family and give up everything to be with me. This was the greatest proof of love that she could have given me. Choosing Shanas as my partner is the one and only great thing that I have done so far in my life. She is my friend, my wife, my confidante. She bravely supports me in all my unconventional quirks. She is my guardian angel, my *molha banu*.

While I was still on the phone, something struck me. Rather than wonder about the place I was going to go to, I suddenly thought about the people I was soon going to leave behind. I worried about my brother who had been abducted because of me in the camps, I thought about his children; about my parents who had been suffering from chronic illnesses for many years. My people needed me and so did my friends and my colleagues. I had no desire to leave them in Bangladesh. It hurt me a lot. Why wasn't there another way to safety? Why couldn't I be free, surrounded by the people I loved, like everyone else?

The weeks that followed this news were the most emotionally intense moments of my life. I had to inform my parents that I was leaving over a phone call. My father and brothers were excited; my mother, as she often did, started to cry. She insisted that I give her one last thing, a shirt of mine. 'I will be able to smell your scent when I miss you after you are gone. I have your photographs for my eyes. Your shirt is to soothe my soul, my son.' I was shattered, literally, into pieces. I wanted to both be with my mother and in Canada. I tried to remain positive, as always, by imagining our reunion one day in the distant country that I was preparing to go to. She would be able to once again take in my scent – no longer that of her invisible son, who had to hide his identity and culture, but that of a free man.

Leaving your family to save your life, knowing that you might never see them again, is the toughest internal conflict that a man can face. I was a father now, and I needed to stay strong, hide my tears and pretend to smile for the sake of my daughter and wife, who was also leaving everything behind, just for me.

Our suitcases had been packed for a long time, but I checked them one last time to ensure that I hadn't forgotten anything. I kept a few photographs of my family to keep them close to me. I put aside the documents that I was able to save from the fires of the genocide and all my notebooks, which contained testimonies of the survivors and proof of the things that my people had endured. I carefully folded my traditional shirts and longyis to proudly wear them in Canada, where people would not object to my costume and culture. I would be able say that I was not only a Rohingya but also a Burmese in my own right.

On 25 August 2021 – four years to the day that our genocide began – an agent of the International Organization of Migration (IOM) waited below our building to usher in the end of our clandestine life and drive us to Dhaka. When we closed the door of our apartment it was as if we were bidding farewell to our hiding place – as if everything was vanishing all of a sudden, though the memories of these past two years would forever remain etched in my mind. Shanas sat in the back with Inayah, I on the front seat. I watched them in the rear-view mirror. We didn't have to speak to each other. I stared at the Bangladeshi sky, blending into Myanmar. Was this going to be the last time I saw it? No, I refused to admit that to myself. One day, I would return.

As we travelled along the bumpy road, I observed the landscape: long, verdant rice paddies, the wild plains, vendors lining the edges of villages with their fruit and vegetable stalls, multitudes of perpetually honking local taxis, newspaper vendors running to car windows to earn a few pennies, women wearing saris of every colour. I thought of my mother and a part of my heart wanted to halt everything to kiss her one last time, to take her along with me so that she too could find peace. But it was impossible. I had wanted to visit the camps before my departure, but I wasn't allowed. I could have been arrested, shattering my dream.

Upon arriving in Dhaka, the IOM agent dropped us off at a hotel where we completed our PCR tests. The following day, we were invited to the office of the

Canadian High Commissioner to Bangladesh. Everything was grand, beautiful and clean. Drinks and food were arranged for us. 'Welcome, my fellow Canadian,' the commissioner announced cheerfully. I couldn't believe my ears. This man who I was meeting for the first time in my life considered me to be one of his own. In my country, nobody had ever said this to me. It was one of the most beautiful moments of my life to feel like I belonged to a country – to exist, to be recognized. All my dreams were finally coming true. Before leaving, I was asked to sign the visitor's book. I didn't know what to write under my address. 'You can note down your Canadian address. It's your new home!' Four years after my exile, I had finally found a new refuge, a new home. For the first time, I felt wanted.

The next day, at the Dhaka airport, all the people who had helped us over the past two years were present to make sure that nothing went wrong. Despite this, we had a final scare. Once we cleared the security check, some agents stopped us and demanded to see our passports. We only had one travel document, a pass from the Department of Immigration and Passports. Although the minister had already informed them of our departure, the agents couldn't resist humiliating us to show us that we were nothing. I was scared that everything would end. After several hours, we were finally able to board the airplane. It was my first time on a plane – the aircraft was gigantic. I held my wife's hand, Inayah in my arms, and whispered to them, 'That's it, hell is over my darlings. A new world is opening up to us. I promise you, now you will never be afraid again.'

Today, on 22 October 2021, I am writing the last few lines of this book. I started *Eradication* as a frightened child and am finishing it as a father. But most importantly, as a free man. Even so, I haven't forgotten anything; especially not my family, my people and my country. In Myanmar, minorities are now standing together as one against the junta. Only this solidarity can guarantee the freedom of the Burmese people.

After the military uprising, the National Unity Government of Myanmar (NUG) – a government in exile – was created by former NLD MPs who managed to escape arbitrary arrests. Its spokesperson and a close friend of Aung San Suu Kyi, Dr Sasa, has publicly stated, 'We support our Rohingya brothers and sisters 100 per cent. Our principles are founded on freedom for all, including the Rohingyas, we would like to see them return to their homes and join us. We are the same people, the same family. Gone are those days when we used to distinguish people based on their colour, ethnicity or religion. The Rohingyas will regain their nationality.'

We had long dreamed of hearing this message from

Aung San Suu Kyi. Burmese activists finally dare to take our names and recognize our rights only now that she has fallen from power and been imprisoned. Being complicit and talking to those who have our blood on their hands is not the solution. It never was, and the coup proved that it will never be. It is better to accept this than submit to it.

The NUG is committed to bringing those responsible for crimes against the Rohingyas to justice. This national reunification is the first step towards building the nation and preserving justice and peace for ethnic minorities in Burma. In the refugee camps of Cox's Bazar, more than a million Rohingyas are waiting to return home. We want a government that recognizes our identity and our right to citizenship, political inclusion and equal treatment. The only hope for Burmese people today is the NUG and international justice. The ICC opened an investigation into the crimes committed against our people in November 2019. We are waiting for our executioners to be punished. This process will probably take several years, but I want to believe in it.

I have grown up witnessing Rohingya fathers – from my grandfather to my older brothers – worry about the safety and future of their daughters. They fear that they will not be able to study, that they won't find good and respectable husbands because they cannot afford a handsome dowry. They are terrified that their daughters will be abducted to the forest at night and raped by Burmese military forces. I never wanted to harbour such fears as a father and now I no longer have to. I know that my daughter will grow up in a different world, free of violence and submission.

But my departure does not signal the end of my fight. Four years after the genocide began, our persecutors are still living with impunity. Worse still, they are now running Myanmar. How much longer will they kill without anyone taking action against them? In Bangladesh, attempts are being made to suppress the resistance. Before shooting my friend Mohib Ullah, his assassins shouted, 'There is no such thing as a Rohingya leader!' They wanted to make an example of him, to tell others: If you continue to speak out, we will kill you. As proof of this, seven refugees who had condemned the crime were killed on the night of 21–22 October.

These people are killing us, but they do not know our strength. We have survived everything and our spirit remains awake; our culture has been liberated and travelled far and wide, even as we live through the cruelest hours in our history. We will resist at all costs and ultimately prevail. We will return home. I will continue to write for my people, to make their voices heard so that justice is done. Now more than ever. And I will honour the promise made to my grandfather, hoping that one day I will take my daughter to the land of her ancestors so that she can know what it means to be a Rohingya.

Over the past two years, every attempt has been made to erase the lines of this book; to silence me and ensure that I continue to live in hiding. The publication of *Eradication* proves that I will never remain silent – that nothing can stop me from fulfilling my destiny and fighting for the rights of my people. After the Rwandan genocide against the Tutsi in 1994 the world declared, 'Never again'. Yet our genocide happened before its eyes. The world has failed us. We should not let this happen again. As a survivor, I do not want others like me to experience the taste of erasure ever again.

A letter to my daughter, My Inayah, my princess

WHEN I STARTED WRITING this book, you weren't yet born and I had never imagined that God would give me the greatest gift of all by blessing me with a child like you. When I was born, my grandfather placed my umbilical cord in a pot and buried it in my country, Myanmar. With that, I belonged to the land – it became my land. This is our tradition. Every father and grandfather observes the same ritual when a child is born.

My grandfather always told me that I needed to do the same for my children. I often imagined it. When my nephews and nieces were born, my brothers buried their pots in our garden, on our lands. But our story ... this story is a little sad, my daughter. Our own Myanmar first seized our lands, then erased our culture and killed our people. All those pots have disappeared, as though we don't exist anymore. I had to flee as well, to escape death. I dream of seeing my land once more before I die. I dream of seeing you running in our fields, your bare feet touching the fresh grass.

When you were born in Bangladesh – where I had fled to – I carried a jar in my bag when I took your mother to the hospital. I promised myself that I would continue our ritual, but the doctors wouldn't give me your umbilical cord. So instead, I give you this book, so that you never forget your history. The history that some Burmese people want to erase. That which I am passing on to you as your legacy. That which I want you to continue. This poem is for you and for all those who share my story.

'This is me, a Rohingya'
When I was born,
I was not a baby like you are
Without a birth certificate,
Just like death.
When I was one,
I was not a child like you are
Without a nation,
Just like a pet.
When I was at school,
I was not a student like you are
Without a Burmese face,
Just like the bleakness of the future.

When I was in another village,
I was not a resident like you are
Seeking approval overnight,
Just like a crazed detainee.
When I pass through my town,
I'm not a citizen like you are,
Holding Form-4 authorization,
Just like a nomad.
When I go to university,
I'm not a fresher like you are
No professionalism and major
Just like illegitimate.
When I approach people,
I'm not acceptable like you are,
Suffering apartheid and chauvinism
Just like quarantine.
When I want to marry,
I'm not a fiancé like you are
Approved for marriage,
Just like an alien.
When I want to repair my hut,
I'm not allowed to like you are
Facing palpable denials,
Just like an invader.
When I arrange a little trade,
I'm not a vendor like you are

Ongoing restricted and confiscated, just like a pauper.
When I apply for the civil service,
I'm not a candidate like you are
Receiving the motive of rejection,
Just like someone segregated.
When hospitalized in the state-run clinic,
I'm not the favorite patient like you are
Marginalized and discriminated,
Just like an outsider.
When I choose religion,
I'm not faithful like you are
Restricted worship in demolished mosques,
Just inhuman.
While I'm in the orchestrated riot,
I'm not a survivor like you are
No assurance of safety,
Just like a rape victim.
When the New Year turns,
I'm not a civilian like you are
Under decades-long operations,
Just like an inventory-item.
Even when I breath the sky's air,
I'm not human like you are,
Without a reliable undertaker,
Just like a loner.
Even when I watch the sunrise,

I'm not living like you are
Without the fertility of hope I live,
Just like a sandcastle.
Despite living on the apex of inhumanity
And the direness of immorality,
I'm quite surrounded.
My skin trembles
Even when I live in the country where I was born,
I can't name it as mine like you do
Without identity,
Just like an immigrant.
Just to feel once the full meaning of freedom
My heart wishes
Just to walk once like in my own world.
Nowadays, no one is like me,
Only myself,
Just a Rohingya !

Acknowledgements

I THANK MY CO-AUTHOR, Emilie Lopes, who believed in me and wanted my book to be published by Éditions Grasset. This work would have been impossible without her help. I am profoundly grateful to her for the support, advice and courage she gave me every day to finish this book. Throughout these years of writing, she has not only been my friend and confidante, but she has also reignited the hope that I have lost a few times. She is now among the most wonderful people I have by my side.

My humble thanks to all my friends and colleagues who have encouraged me to take up my pen, starting with Aye Tun @ Dilwar Kamaal, a good friend and precious voice whom I listen to and admire.

I extend my heartfelt thanks to all the international experts who saw my potential and commitment over the decades. A special mention for the Action Against Hunger teams that I worked with in Arakan, who consistently encouraged me to write. I am thinking especially of

Sophie Renault, Andrew Riley, Adam Tousley, Kristen Etnoyer, Pramudith Rupasinghe and Valerie Waters, a psychologist who was always proud of me for being a devoted colleague and friend. Her staff still remembers her as one of the best and most praiseworthy managers they have ever had.

Thanks also to Juliette Joste, who has been more than just an editor throughout these years of writing. She dedicated herself to doing everything she could to ensure that I could leave Bangladesh. I shall never forget her commitment, nor that of Olivier Nora, to whom I owe a great deal. I also thank Simon Labrosse and all the teams at Éditions Grasset who have ensured that this book sees the light of day.

My sincere gratitude to Matt Wells, of the UNHCR team in Dhaka, to Benoit Préfontaine, to Alex Neve and to all the other people who have supported me, personally and professionally, and have brought me towards the path of freedom so I could publish this book.

A final thank you to my beloved parents and to my spouse. Without the constant support and true blessings of my parents, and the unwavering faith of my wife, nothing would be the same and nothing would be possible. And to Inayah, my gift from God.

Bibliography

Amnesty International, 'Myanmar: Government fails to protect Rohingya after world court order', 22 May 2020. Available at: https://www.amnesty.org/en/latest/news/2020/05/myanmar-government-fails-to-protect-rohingya-after-world-court-order/.

———. *Myanmar: The Rohingya Minority: Fundamental rights denied*, 2004.

Aung San Suu Kyi, *Freedom From Fear* (London: Penguin, 1991).

Fortify Rights, 'ARSA: End Abductions, Torture, Threats Against Rohingya Refugees and Women Aid Workers', 14 March 2019. Available at: https://www.fortifyrights.org/mya-inv-2019-03-14/.

———. *'They Gave Them Long Swords'*, 2018.

Human Rights Watch, *'All You Can Do is Pray': Crimes Against Humanity and Ethnic Cleansing of Rohingya Muslims in Burma's Arakan State*, 2013.

———. 'Burma: Army Report Whitewashes Ethnic Cleansing', 14 November 2017. Available at: https://

www.hrw.org/news/2017/11/14/burma-army-report-whitewashes-ethnic-cleansing.

———. *'Nothing Called Freedom': A Decade of Detention for Rohingya in Myanmar's Rakhine State*, 2022.

Independent International Fact-Finding Mission on Myanmar, *Report to the 42nd session of the Human Rights Council*, 2019.

James Byrne and Shehzar Doja (eds.), *I am a Rohingya: Poetry from the Camps and Beyond* (Lancashire: Arc Publications, 2019).

Mayyu Ali, *The Blossom* (Cox's Bazaar: self-published, 2018).

———. *Exodus: between genocide and me* (Bangladesh: self-published, 2019).

Public sitting held on 10 December 2019: Hearings on Application of the Convention on the Prevention and Punishment of the Crime of Genocide (The Gambia v. Myanmar: 11 States intervening) (statement of Abubacarr Marie Tambadou, Minister of Justice of Gambia).

Rebecca Wright, Katie Hunt and Joshua Berlinger, 'Aung San Suu Kyi breaks silence on Rohingya, sparks storm of criticism', *CNN*, 19 September 2017. Available at: https://edition.cnn.com/2017/09/18/asia/aung-san-suu-kyi-speech-rohingya.

Ro Mayyu Ali, 'Open letter from a Rohingya to Aung San Suu Kyi', *Al Jazeera*, 14 October 2017. Available at: https://www.aljazeera.com/news/2017/10/14/open-letter-from-a-rohingya-to-aung-san-suu-kyi.

Thea Forbes, 'Aung San Suu Kyi condemns sexual violence in conflict', *Burma News International*, 25 May 2011. Available at: https://www.bnionline.net/en/mizzima-news/item/10806-aung-san-suu-kyi-condemns-sexual-violence-in-conflict.html.

The State Peace and Development Council, Law No. 10/2010, 'The National Anthem Law', 21 October 2010. Available at: https://www.burmalibrary.org/docs18/2010-10-21-SPDC_Law2010-10_National_Anthem_Law-oag-en.pdf.

UNHCR, 'Rohingya emergency', updated April 2025. Available at: https://www.unhcr.org/emergencies/rohingya-emergency.

Voice of America, 'Myanmar Poets Square Off Against Junta's War on Words', 4 June 2021. Available at: https://www.voanews.com/a/east-asia-pacific_myanmar-poets-square-against-juntas-war-words/6206646.html.